Maths

Assessment Practice

Book 1

Ages 9–10 Year 5

Andy Baines

OXFORD
UNIVERSITY PRESS

OXFORD
UNIVERSITY PRESS

Great Clarendon Street, Oxford, OX2 6DP, United Kingdom

Oxford University Press is a department of the University of Oxford.
It furthers the University's objective of excellence in research, scholarship,
and education by publishing worldwide. Oxford is a registered trade mark
of Oxford University Press in the UK and in certain other countries

British Library Cataloguing in Publication Data
Data available

978-1-382-05398-3

10 9 8 7 6 5 4 3 2 1

Printed in the UK

The manufacturing process conforms to the environmental
regulations of the country of origin

Acknowledgements

Content Development Adviser: Jane Cooney
Page make-up: QBS
Cover illustrations: Lo Cole
Illustrations: QBS and Tech-Set Limited

Although we have made every effort to trace and contact
all copyright holders before publication this has not been
possible in all cases. If notified, the publisher will rectify
any errors or omissions at the earliest opportunity.

Contents

Welcome

The 11+ exam is used by grammar schools and selective independent schools for entrance into Year 7. It assesses a child in verbal, non-verbal, English and mathematical reasoning, although individual schools may not test all four subjects, and they may combine some of the subjects together. The 11+ covers English and maths topics that a child will be familiar with from the National Curriculum, but supplements these with verbal reasoning and non-verbal reasoning questions.

Bond offers a complete, flexible programme of preparation materials that you can adapt to your child's specific needs and to the requirements of the exam, or exams.

Do remember to keep checking in with your school of choice so that you know which exam they are using. Schools change their exam boards from time to time. When sitting the actual test, there may be an additional time allowance for candidates needing additional support or an exam in a different format, so do also check with your prospective school if your child needs this. Every child has the right to access the 11+ exam and schools will do all that they can to support them.

Is This Book for a Specific Exam Board?

Unless signalled on the front cover as being geared towards a specific exam board, all Bond 11+ Maths materials are designed to hone the flexibility of approach essential to overcoming the challenges of any 11+ exam. They are also useful preparation for Key Stage 2 SATS exams. The Bond system provides learning, information, and consolidation so that children have an extended, rich education. Our aim is to familiarise children with the type of questions they will find in the exam and to give them the transferable skills that will allow a child to attempt any question in any exam.

As different exam boards and schools may have different question types, the 11+ can be challenging to prepare for. This book can be used as preparation for all exam boards as it provides a wide selection of question types and an enriched education is the best preparation.

We help children to both master the techniques and develop the logic and rationale to tackle any unknown question types.

If your child has been working towards an exam from a specific exam board and then the board used by your chosen school changes, all is not lost. This book is good preparation for whichever exam board is being used and the skills covered can be applied to any 11+ exam or independent school entrance exam. It is equally useful for pupils just looking for an extra challenge or wishing to prepare for secondary school.

A Note on Question Formats

The majority of 11+ exams now use multiple-choice answer format (where your child chooses their answer from a list of options), either entirely or for most of their questions. In Bond practice materials, your child will encounter both multiple-choice questions and some in 'standard format', which is where they have to write or type the answer into a box. We continue to use both because, whilst on the one hand it is good to practice the format faced in the exam, standard format questions are proven to be more effective for learning and practice. When a child has to decide on an answer themselves without being given options, the simple act of writing out their answer makes their brain work a bit harder and helps those important skills to get stuck in their memory, ready to be used when they sit down for the real test itself.

How Else Can My Child Prepare for the 11+ Exam?

Bond has a wide range of books and resources to support learning. These include flashcards, the *10 Minute Test* books and the *Puzzle* series. Bond Online provides a fun way for your child to consolidate their learning and we offer subscriptions which harness adaptive technology, perfect for building confidence.

KEY STUDY SKILLS

Working towards an entrance exam can be an exciting challenge. It is the chance to learn new things and to prepare for secondary school. Here are some tips to help your child:

- Create a study schedule so that your child has a regular routine.

- Balance short bursts of practice with longer assessment papers.

- Create a quiet study space with pencils, an eraser, paper for working out, books and a notebook for writing down techniques. If they study in different places, keep everything in a box that they can take with you.

- Encourage your child to write down strategies to solve new topics.

- Limit distractions such as television, technology and games when they are studying.

- Remind your child that errors are useful. They are part of the journey to success.

A Note for Parents

Parents have a crucial role in helping children and motivating them. Here are some ways that you can really make a difference.

- Check your child is working at the right level. The goal is being able to score 85% on average. It's demotivating if they can't complete questions. It is also important that they work through the system so they are at the right level for the exam at the right time.

- Mark work promptly and go through errors. If papers have not been marked, a child has no idea how they are doing or whether they are repeating the same mistakes.

- Use the *Bond Handbooks* to help your child understand new techniques.

- Limit the range of homework you give your child. The best results are achieved by a system that gradually increases in difficulty. Completing lots of books and papers doesn't guarantee your child's success and often creates stress.

- If your child is struggling with something specific, add additional support in that area. Use *Bond 10 Minute Tests* for consolidation.

- Communication is key. Encourage your child to focus on the positive. No exam is going to ask for 100%, so pushing for that is unrealistic and stressful.

- If your child is constantly struggling, be realistic about whether a selective education is the right choice at this point in time. Many children move to a selective school for their GCSEs or A levels so not going to a selective school now doesn't mean they never will. It is about finding the best school for your child.

How to Use This Book

This book includes many step-by-step techniques for solving different question types. If further support is needed it can be used alongside one or more of the *Bond Handbooks*, which offer insights into the full range of questions that might occur in the exam.

- The first section of the book is made up of Learning Papers that focus on key skills with worked examples and then lots of questions for consolidation.

- The second section of the book is made up of Mixed Papers so that children continue to consolidate and do not forget what they have learnt.

- The final section includes two full Test Papers, which can be broken down into shorter sections for more focussed practice, or can be used as full mock tests for that all important exam practice.

- There is an 11+ study guide at the back of the book with some useful hints and tips.

- The removable booklet attached to the back cover includes fully worked out answers to explain how an answer has been reached.

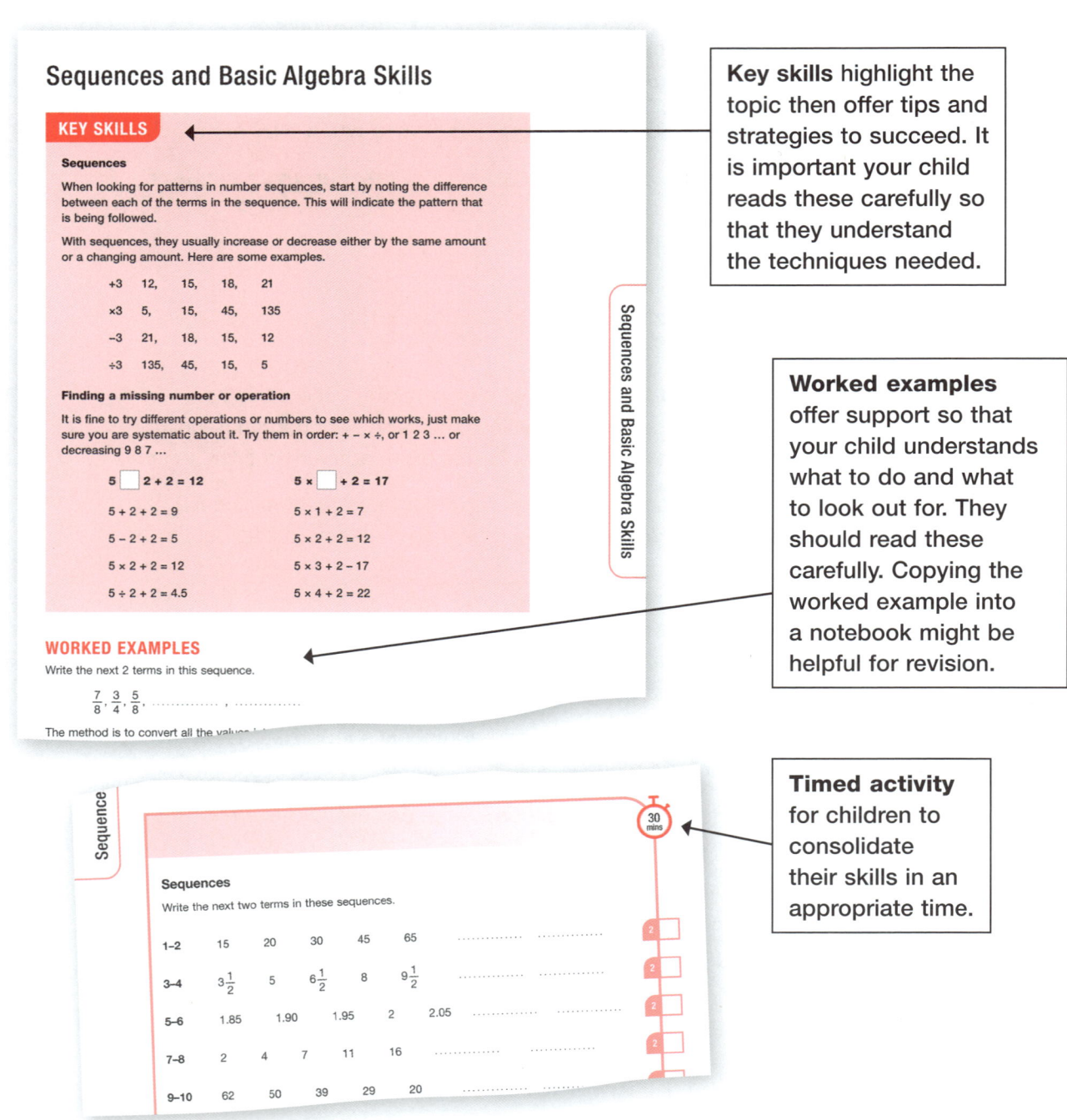

Key skills highlight the topic then offer tips and strategies to succeed. It is important your child reads these carefully so that they understand the techniques needed.

Worked examples offer support so that your child understands what to do and what to look out for. They should read these carefully. Copying the worked example into a notebook might be helpful for revision.

Timed activity for children to consolidate their skills in an appropriate time.

KEY MATHS SKILLS

This Bond 11+ Maths Assessment Practice book is useful for all 11+ exams. The Learning Papers cover the following key skills:

- **Numbers** – adding, subtracting, multiplying and dividing, number lines, writing numbers, place value, order and compare, prime/square/cube numbers and roots, fractions, decimals and percentages, patterns and sequences, word problems.

- **Measurements** – unit conversions, mass, area, length, volume, money, time.

- **Statistics** – line charts, bar charts, pie charts, Venn diagrams, pictograms, averages.

- **Problem solving** – bus or train timetables, logic questions, multi-step problems, ratio and proportion, scale problems.

- **Geometry** – 2D and 3D shapes, area and perimeter of shapes, angles, coordinates, symmetry, translations.

- **Algebra** – BIDMAS, simple algebraic equations, simple substitution.

The Mixed Papers ensure the key skills are consolidated thoroughly, then the Test Papers give children the opportunity to get used to the exam process as a natural progression of each book. Don't forget that a rounded education is key. Get your child used to reading graphs, timetables and charts. They can try doing sudoku and number games, play online games like Tetris, Snake or Road Blocks and do some logic and number puzzles – Bond has a Number Puzzle book to make this more fun. There are plenty of times-tables apps to ensure their basic skills are fast and accurate, and games such as Pet Bingo, Marble Math, and Squeebles Maths Race are great for consolidating skills. Hacker Can is excellent for developing maths and logic skills through learning to program.

Each book is part of the Bond system with books increasing gradually in difficulty. Once your child has completed this book, there is a clear progression in starting the next book age band if you child has an average score of 85% in this book. If they have achieved an average score of 70%–85%, then another book at this same age band they understand will provide further support. If your child has achieved an average score of less than 70%, then moving down an age band will be most useful. Once your child has then developed the skills needed at this lower age band, they can then move up with confidence. It is often better to begin at a lower age band to build confidence as your child learns and develops their 11+ skills.

Basic Number Skills

KEY SKILL

Types of numbers

Factors of a number are numbers that divide into it with no remainder. For example 1, 2, 4 and 8 are all factors of 8.

Multiples are just extended times tables. They are the original number multiplied by another number.

Prime numbers are whole numbers greater than 1 that have only 2 factors: 1 and the number itself.

Composites are numbers that have more than 2 factors, so they can be divided by 1, the number itself and at least 1 other number.

Square numbers are made by multiplying a number by itself.

Cube numbers are made by multiplying a number by itself 3 times.

Powers are the number of times a number is multiplied by itself, for example $3^4 = 3 \times 3 \times 3 \times 3$.

Negative numbers are less than zero and are shown with a minus symbol in front of the number.

	multiples	factors	prime factors	composite	prime	squared number	cubed number
1	1, 2, 3, …	1				1 × 1	1 × 1 × 1
2	2, 4, 6, …	1, 2	2		1 × 2		
3	3, 6, 9, …	1, 3	3		1 × 3		
4	4, 8, 12, …	1, 2, 4	2 × 2	1, 2, 4		2 × 2	
5	5, 10, 15, …	1, 5	5		1 × 5		
6	6, 12, 18, …	1, 2, 3, 6	2 × 3	1, 2, 3, 6			
7	7, 14, 21, …	1, 7	7		1 × 7		
8	8, 16, 24, …	1, 2, 4, 8	2 × 2 × 2	1, 2, 4, 8			2 × 2 × 2
9	9, 18, 27, …	1, 3, 9	3 × 3	1, 3, 9		3 × 3	
10	10, 20, 30, …	1, 2, 5, 10	2 × 5	1, 2, 5, 10			
11							
12							

Complete the table for the numbers 11 and 12 or two other numbers of your choice.

Place value

You need to know the value of a digit wherever it appears in a number.

1234.5 and 0.123 are shown below.

thousands	hundreds	tens	ones	decimal point	tenths	hundredths	thousandths
1	2	3	4	.	5		
			0	.	1	2	3

1234.5 has **3** tens and **5** tenths

0.123 has **0** tens and **1** tenth

WORKED EXAMPLES

The distance from London to Sydney is 19 625 miles.

This is approximately . . . . miles to the nearest 1000 miles, ... miles

to the nearest 100 miles and . . . . miles to the nearest 10 miles.

To answer 'to the nearest' questions, you will need to round numbers. Rounding is the process of simplifying a number to make calculations easier. If the digit being rounded to is followed by a digit that is 5 or more, it increases by 1. If it is followed by a digit that is 4 or less, it stays the same.

19 625 miles to the nearest 1000 miles: **20 000**.

19 625 miles to the nearest 100 miles: **19 600**.

19 625 miles to the nearest 10 miles: **19 630**. (In the middle, so round up.)

Place Value

Here are 6 numbers: 32   27   *35*   33   *26*   29

handwritten: 3 35 × 26 210 700

1 Find the largest number and multiply it by the smallest. *9.1.0* — **1**

2 What is the biggest number you can make with these digits? **3, 6, 4, 8, 3, 2**

handwritten: 832   864 332 — **1**

3 Write in figures the number ten thousand and fourteen. *10,014* — **1**

4 Write in figures the number one hundred and one thousand. *101,000* — **1**

Rounding

5 What is 8536 to the nearest 1000? *8536 = 9000* — **1**

6 What is 8536 to the nearest 100? *8536 = 8500* — **1**

7 What is 7680 rounded to the nearest 1000? *7680 = 8000* — **1**

8 Round 4535 to the nearest 10. *4535 = 4540* — **1**

Factors

Write in the missing numbers which complete the pairs of factors.

9 The pairs of factors of 14 are 1 and 14, 2 and ...*7*... — **1**

10–12
    The pairs of factors of 18 are 1 and ...*18*......., ... and ....,
    3 and 6. — **3**

Multiples

13–16

Write down all the numbers between 30 and 60 which are multiples of 8.

32,40,48,52

[4]

Primes

23

17 What is the total of the first 4 prime numbers? *2,3,5,7,13,17,31,37*

[1]

18 What is the difference between the prime numbers that are more than 20 and less than 30?

31 and 37 = 6

[1]

19 What is the difference between the prime numbers that are more than 30 and less than 40?

31 and 37 = 7

[1]

Negative Numbers

20 What number is the arrow pointing to below? *2.5*

- + -4 +5 = 1

21–22

It was −4°C yesterday, today it is 2 degrees colder, but tomorrow it will warm up by 3 degrees.

-4 -2 = -6 -3

The temperature today is ......*-6*...°C and tomorrow it will be ....*3*....°C.

[2]

Square Numbers

23 What is 8 squared? ..... *8×8 = 64*

[1]

24 What is 11^2? ..... *11×11 = 121*

[1]

9^2

25 Which number multiplied by itself gives 81? .....

[1]

Total
25

Using the Four Operations

KEY SKILLS

Short division

With short division it is important to work in columns and spread your work out. Then it is easier to see what you are doing.

WORKED EXAMPLES

Division

$6\overline{)2\ 8\ 0\ 6}$

6 does not divide into 2, so place a **0** above the 2 so that you know you have dealt with that.

0
$6\overline{)2\ 8\ 0\ 6}$

6 divides into 40 six times, remainder 4; 46 = 6 × 6 + 4, so place a **6** above the 0 and place the **4** in front of the next digit, 6.

0 4
$6\overline{)2\ 8\ 40\ 6}$

6 divides into 40 six times, remainder 4; 46 = 6 × 6 + 4, so place a **6** above the 0 and place the **4** in front of the next digit, 6.

0 4 6
$6\overline{)2\ 8\ 40\ 46}$

6 divides into 46 seven times, remainder 4; 46 = 6 × 7 + 4, so place a **7** above the 6 and place the **4** as the remainder because there are no more digits to divide.

0 4 6 7 r4
$6\overline{)2\ 8\ 40\ 46}$

So 2806 ÷ 6 = **467 r4**

Addition and subtraction

With addition and subtraction of decimals, you can ignore the decimal point then add it back in.

The only rule here is that in both numbers you must have the same number of digits after the decimal point. For example, 7 − 0.04 = 7.00 − 0.04 and 3.4 + 5.01 = 3.40 + 5.01

There are several methods for doing the subtraction; use which ever you find easiest.

The following example uses the borrow and pay back method.

$$\begin{array}{r} 9{\cdot}25 \\ -\ 0{\cdot}98 \\ \hline \end{array}$$

Ignore the decimal points.

$$\begin{array}{r} 925 \\ -\ 98 \\ \hline \end{array}$$

Start on the right looking at the units first, then look at the tens and last the hundreds.

You can take 5 from 8, but not 8 from 5.

You can take 8 from 15 though. So borrow 10 from the top row of the column to the left to do 15 – 8. Pay back 10 to the bottom row of that column.

$$\begin{array}{r} 9\,2\,{}^{1}5 \\ -\ {}_{1}9\,8 \\ \hline 7 \end{array}$$

You then have 20 – 90, but you need to repay the 10, so change this to 20 – 90 – 10. But this can't be done. So borrow 100 from the top row of the column to the left to do 120 – 90 – 10. Pay back the 100 that you borrowed by putting it in the bottom row of the column to the left.

$$\begin{array}{r} 9\,{}^{1}2\,{}^{1}5 \\ -\ {}_{1}0\,{}_{1}9\,8 \\ \hline 2\,7 \end{array}$$

Then 900 – 100 = 800, and add the decimal point back in.

$$\begin{array}{r} 9\,{}^{1}2\,{}^{1}5 \\ -\ {}_{1}0\,{}_{1}9\,8 \\ \hline 8{\cdot}2\,7 \end{array}$$

Long multiplication

With long multiplication it is important that you deal with each of the second number's digits one at a time.

$$\begin{array}{r} 476 \\ \times\ 532 \\ \hline \end{array}$$

476	
× 532	
800	400 × 2
140	70 × 2
12	6 × 2
12000	400 × 30
2100	70 × 30
180	6 × 30
20000	400 × 500
35000	70 × 500
+ 3000	6 × 500

476	
× 532	
952	
14280	
238000	
25³3¹2³32	

30 mins

Addition

Use this calculation to help you answer questions 1–3.

```
    98
+   76
   174
```

1
```
   198
+   76
```

2
```
   398
+   76
```

3
```
   498
+  176
```

4
```
   4.68
   9.25
+  3.79
```

5
```
   14.37
+  11.70
```

Subtraction

Underline the correct answer for question 6.

6 1.00 – 0.9 =   0.01   1.9   1.1   0.1

7 Take forty-nine from two thousand and ten. ....

8   4.12
       − 2.76

       _____

9 Take four hundred and thirty-nine from seven thousand five hundred. Write the answer in figures.

       . . . .

10

Multiplication

11 What are four sixes?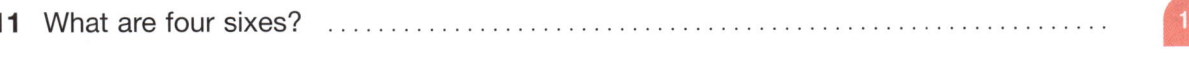

12 Find three lots of nine.

13 Seven times eight is

14   145
       × 308

       _____

15   6.17
       ×   8
       ─────
       49·3 6

Division

16–18

Fill in the missing numbers.

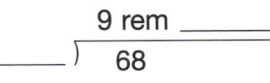

     8 rem 2   9 rem _____
6)‾‾‾‾‾‾‾‾‾   _____)‾‾ 68

   _____

19   6) 27.92   [1]

20–21 Underline the calculations that have a remainder of 3.   [2]

29 ÷ 5   21 ÷ 6   19 ÷ 4   28 ÷ 7

Mixed operations

> **TOP TIP!**
> Use columns to make sure you are not mixing hundreds with ones or tens.

22 Add half of 8 to twice 6. ....   [1]

Find the answers to these calculations.

23 1997 + 455 = ...   [1]

24 4557 – 994 = ...   [1]

The **product** of 2 numbers is 42. One of the numbers is 7.

25 What is the other number? ....   [1]

Total
25

Fractions, Decimals and Percentages

KEY SKILLS

Equivalent fractions

Always multiply or divide both the numerator (the top number) and the denominator (the bottom number) by the same number to find an equivalent fraction.

$$\frac{2}{7} = \frac{2 \times 2}{2 \times 7} = \frac{3 \times 2}{3 \times 7} = \frac{4 \times 2}{4 \times 7} = \frac{5 \times 2}{5 \times 7}$$

$$\frac{2}{7} = \frac{4}{14} = \frac{6}{21} = \frac{8}{28} = \frac{10}{35}$$

$$\frac{10}{35} = \frac{10 \div 5}{35 \div 5} = \frac{2}{7}$$

Fraction of a number

Convert the number into a fraction, then multiply the numerators and denominators before cancelling down.

$$\frac{2}{7} \text{ of } 28 = \frac{2}{7} \times 28 = \frac{2}{7} \times \frac{28}{1} = \frac{2 \times 28}{7 \times 1} = \frac{2 \times 7 \times 4}{7 \times 1} = \frac{2 \times 4}{1} = 8$$

Sometimes there are shorter methods, but this will always work.

Multiplying, dividing and ordering decimals

To multiply by 10, first place the number in a decimal grid using hundreds, tens, ones, tenths, hundredths, thousandths, etc.

H	T	O	.	t	h	th	hth
		0	.	0	0	3	5

Multiply a number by 10 by moving it one place to the left.

H	T	O	.	t	h	th	hth
		0	.	0	0	3	5
		0	.	0	3	5	

Multiply it by 100 by moving it two places to the left.

H	T	O	..	t	h	th	hth
		0	.	0	0	3	5
		0	.	3	5		

Here are some examples

0.0035×10	= 0.035		81.4×10	= 814
0.0035×100	= 0.35		81.4×100	= 8140
0.0035×1000	= 3.5		81.4×1000	= 81 400

To divide a number by 10, place the number in a decimal grid again and then move it one place to the right. To divide the number by 100 move it two places to the right on the grid.

To order decimal numbers use a decimal grid again. Place the decimal point in a column first then fill the numbers in afterwards and add in any extra 0s. This is how the following numbers would work in the grid: 0.48, 0.379, 2.012.

H	T	O	.	t	h	th	Order (largest first)
		0	.	4	8	0	second
		0	.	3	7	9	third
		2	.	0	1	2	first

Equivalent decimals and percentages of $\frac{1}{2}, \frac{1}{4}, \frac{1}{5}, \frac{2}{5}, \frac{4}{5}$

Here are the equivalent decimals and percentages for these fractions.

$$\frac{1}{2} = \frac{50 \times 1}{50 \times 2} = \frac{50}{100} = 50\% = 0.50 = 0.5$$

$$\frac{1}{4} = \frac{25 \times 1}{25 \times 4} = \frac{25}{100} = 25\% = 0.25$$

$$\frac{1}{5} = \frac{20 \times 1}{20 \times 5} = \frac{20}{100} = 20\% = 0.20 = 0.2$$

$$\frac{2}{5} = \frac{20 \times 2}{20 \times 5} = \frac{40}{100} = 40\% = 0.40 = 0.4$$

$$\frac{4}{5} = \frac{20 \times 4}{20 \times 5} = \frac{80}{100} = 80\% = 0.80 = 0.8$$

In an **improper fraction** the number on top (the numerator) is the same as or greater than the number on the bottom (the denominator). The numerator shows how many pieces there are. The denominator shows how many pieces make up a whole.

WORKED EXAMPLES

- Change these improper fractions into **mixed numbers** in their **lowest terms**:

$$\frac{14}{10}, \frac{32}{5}.$$

First work out how many whole numbers there are in the improper fraction and what the remainder is. You do this by finding how many times the denominator will go into the numerator.

$$\frac{14}{10} = \frac{10 + 4}{10} = \frac{10}{10} + \frac{4}{10} = 1 + \frac{4}{10}$$

Then cancel the numbers on the top and bottom of the fraction to change it to its lowest terms. Here, both 4 and 10 can be divided by 2:

$$1 + \frac{4}{10} = 1 + \frac{2 \times 2}{2 \times 5} = 1\frac{2}{5}$$

The answer is $\frac{14}{10} = 1\frac{2}{5}$.

$$\frac{32}{5} = \frac{30+2}{5} = \frac{30}{5} + \frac{2}{5} = 6 + \frac{2}{5} = 6\frac{2}{5}$$

The answer is $\frac{32}{5} = \mathbf{6\frac{2}{5}}$. Note that $\frac{2}{5}$ is already in its lowest terms.

- Change these mixed numbers into improper fractions in their lowest terms:

$$1\frac{4}{10}, 6\frac{2}{5}.$$

For $1\frac{4}{10}$ first change the mixed number into tenths. Multiply the whole number (1) by the denominator (10) and add the remainder to make it into an equivalent fraction. In tenths, $1\frac{4}{10}$ is the same as $\frac{14}{10}$.

$$1\frac{4}{10} = 1 + \frac{4}{10} = \frac{10}{10} + \frac{4}{10} = \frac{10+4}{10} = \frac{14}{10}$$

To put $\frac{14}{10}$ into its lowest terms, find the biggest number that will divide evenly into both the numerator and the denominator. In this case that number is 2: $14 \div 2 = 7$ and $10 \div 2 = 5$.

$$\frac{14}{10} = \frac{2 \times 7}{2 \times 5} = \mathbf{\frac{7}{5}}$$

For $6\frac{2}{5}$ split up the mixed numbers and turn them into fifths. Multiply the whole number (6) by the denominator (5) to find the numerator. 6 is the same as $\frac{30}{5}$. So $6\frac{2}{5}$ is $\frac{32}{5}$ in its lowest terms.

$$6\frac{2}{5} = 6 + \frac{2}{5} = \frac{30}{5} + \frac{2}{5} = \frac{30+2}{5} = \mathbf{\frac{32}{5}}$$

- Convert $\frac{13}{25}, \frac{7}{10}, \frac{52}{75}$ into decimals and percentages.

Firstly convert the fractions so each has a denominator of 100.

Look to multiply both the numerator and denominator by 10 if the denominator is a multiple of 10, or by 4 if the denominator is a multiple of 25. Then divide to get the denominator to 100. Here are some examples.

$$\frac{3}{25} = \frac{4 \times 3}{4 \times 25} = \frac{12}{100}$$

The denominator is 25, so multiply both the numerator and the denominator by 4.

$$\frac{3}{25} = \frac{2 \times 3}{2 \times 50} = \frac{6}{100}$$

The denominator is 50, you can multiply both the numerator and the denominator by 2 to get the denominator to 100 in one step.

$$\frac{3}{75} = \frac{4 \times 3}{4 \times 75} = \frac{12}{300} = \frac{12 \div 3}{300 \div 3} = \frac{4}{100}$$

Multiply both the numerator and the denominator by 4. In order to get the denominator to 100 we have to divide 300 by 3. Divide the numerator by 3 as well. The answer is $\frac{4}{100}$

$$\frac{3}{10} = \frac{10 \times 3}{10 \times 10} = \frac{30}{100}$$

The denominator is 10, so multiply both the numerator and the denominator by 10.

$$\frac{3}{20} = \frac{5 \times 3}{5 \times 20} = \frac{15}{100}$$

The denominator is 20, you can multiply both the numerator and the denominator by 5 to get the denominator to 100 in one step.

$$\frac{8}{40} = \frac{10 \times 8}{10 \times 40} = \frac{80}{400} = \frac{80 \div 4}{400 \div 4} = \frac{20}{100}$$

The denominator is a multiple of 10, so multiply both the numerator and the denominator by 10. In order to get the denominator to 100 we have to divide both the numerator and the denominator by 4. The answer is $\frac{20}{100}$.

The next step is to change the fraction into a percentage. You have to find the equivalent fraction with a denominator of 100. The numerator will give you the percentage.

In the following example, multiplying 25 (the denominator) by 4 gives us 100. Then by multiplying 13 (the numerator) by 4 as well we get $\frac{52}{100}$. When 52 is divided by 100 we get 0.52 or 52%.

$$\frac{13}{25} = \frac{4 \times 13}{4 \times 25} = \frac{52}{100} = 0 \cdot 52 = 52\%$$

$$\frac{7}{10} = \frac{7 \times 10}{10 \times 10} = \frac{70}{100} = 0 \cdot 70 = 70\%$$

$$\frac{51}{75} = \frac{4 \times 51}{4 \times 75} = \frac{204}{300} = \frac{204 \div 3}{300 \div 3} = 0 \cdot 68 = 68\%$$

30 mins

Equivalent Fractions

Complete these fractions.

1 $\frac{2}{10} = \frac{4}{}$

2 $\frac{5}{5} = \frac{}{7}$

3 $\frac{3}{6} = \frac{4}{}$

3

Adding/Subtracting Fractions

Write the answers to these fraction calculations in the lowest terms.

4 $\frac{2}{10} + \frac{7}{10} - \frac{1}{10} =$ ....

1

5 $\frac{9}{10} - \frac{6}{10} + \frac{2}{10} =$ ....

1

6 $\frac{9}{100} + \frac{90}{100} =$ ....

1

Identifying Fractions (Including Simplifying)

What fraction of each shape is shaded or plain?

7

Shaded .... `1` ☐

8

Shaded .... `1` ☐

9

Shaded .... `1` ☐

Improper Fractions and Mixed Numbers

10 = ... halves `1` ☐

11 $1\frac{3}{4}$ = ... quarters `1` ☐

Fraction of a Number

In a school, $\frac{3}{5}$ of the pupils were boys and there were 240 girls.

12 How many boys were in the school? .... `1` ☐

13 How many children were in the school? .... `1` ☐

There are 720 books in the school library.

14 How many books has John read if he has read one-twelfth of them? .... `1` ☐

Ordering Decimals

Indicate which is larger by writing < or > in each space.

15 £13.07 .... £13.60 `1` ☐

16 €9.90 .... €9.78 `1` ☐

Multiplying and Dividing Decimals by 10, 100 and 1000

Multiply each of these numbers by 100.

17 0.24 .... `1` ☐

18 0.0076 .... `1` ☐

Money Conversion

TOP TIP!

Convert money into the same units, either all £ or all p.

19 20p × .... = £1.00 `1` ☐

20 50p × .... = £2.00 `1` ☐

21 10p × .... = £5.00 `1` ☐

Percentages

In my sister's box of counters, 50% of them are green, 25% are blue and the remaining 11 are white counters.

22 How many counters are there altogether? .... `1` ☐

In a village of 550 people, 40% of the population are adults.

23 How many children are there? .... `1` ☐

Mixed Fractions, Decimals and Percentages

Write the following fractions as decimals.

24 $\frac{1}{10}$ = ... `1` ☐

25 $\frac{3}{100}$ = ... `1` ☐

Total 25

Sequences and Basic Algebra Skills

KEY SKILLS

Sequences

When looking for patterns in number sequences, start by noting the difference between each of the terms in the sequence. This will indicate the pattern that is being followed.

With sequences, they usually increase or decrease either by the same amount or a changing amount. Here are some examples.

+3	12,	15,	18,	21
×3	5,	15,	45,	135
−3	21,	18,	15,	12
÷3	135,	45,	15,	5

Finding a missing number or operation

It is fine to try different operations or numbers to see which works, just make sure you are systematic about it. Try them in order: + − × ÷, or 1 2 3 … or decreasing 9 8 7 …

$5 \boxed{} 2 + 2 = 12$

$5 + 2 + 2 = 9$

$5 - 2 + 2 = 5$

$5 \times 2 + 2 = 12$

$5 \div 2 + 2 = 4.5$

$5 \times \boxed{} + 2 = 17$

$5 \times 1 + 2 = 7$

$5 \times 2 + 2 = 12$

$5 \times 3 + 2 - 17$

$5 \times 4 + 2 = 22$

WORKED EXAMPLES

Write the next 2 terms in this sequence.

$$\frac{7}{8}, \frac{3}{4}, \frac{5}{8}, \ldots\ldots\ldots\ldots\ , \ldots\ldots\ldots\ldots$$

The method is to convert all the values into improper fractions with the same denominator before looking for a pattern.

$$\frac{7}{8}, \frac{3 \times 2}{4 \times 2} = \frac{6}{8}, \frac{5}{8},$$

So in this pattern, the denominators stay the same (8) and the numerator is 1 less each time, so $\frac{4}{8}, \frac{3}{8}$, and as $\frac{4}{8} = \frac{1}{2}$, the answer would be $\frac{1}{2}, \frac{3}{8}$.

Missing numbers

I think of a number. I triple it. Then I add 7. The answer is 13. What was the number?

Start with the unknown as a symbol or algebra letter and create an equation to help you work back to the answer.

x	I think of a number.
$3x$	I triple it.
$3x + 7$	I then add 7.
$3x + 7 = 13$	The answer is 13. Find x.

> **TOP TIP!**
>
> $4x$ means 4 times x,
> $3y$ means 3 times y
> and so on.

What number must be multiplied by 3 and added to 7 to give 13? You can often work out the answer by just reversing the operations (swapping + for − and ÷ for ×).

Work backwards through the sum.

Start with 13, then subtract 7 then divide by 3.

$13 - 7 = 6$

$6 \div 3 = 2$

$x = 2$

Always check your answer to make sure. $2 \times 3 + 7 = 13$

---

30 mins

Sequences

Write the next two terms in these sequences.

1–2	15	20	30	45	65	*90* *120* ....
3–4	$3\frac{1}{2}$	5	$6\frac{1}{2}$	8	$9\frac{1}{2}$	*11* *12½* ....
5–6	1.85	1.90	1.95	2	2.05	....
7–8	2	4	7	11	16	....
9–10	62	50	39	29	20	....
11–12	12340	1234	123.4	....	....	

2
2
2
2
2
2

Missing Operations and Missing Numbers

Insert the missing operations from +, −, ×, ÷.

13–14   57 . . . . 3 = 2 17   `2` `☐`

15–16   57 . . . . 13 = 11 4   `2` `☐`

17–18   57 . . . . 3 = 120 2   `2` `☐`

Basic Algebra Skills

19   I think of a number, add 1, divide by 3, and the answer is 2.
What is the number?   . . . .   `1` `☐`

20   I think of a number, divide it by 4 and then add 2.
The answer is 6. What is the number?   . . . .   `1` `☐`

21   When I subtract 4 times a certain number from 50,
the remainder is 6. What is the number?   . . . .   `1` `☐`

22   The sum of two numbers is 43. The smaller number is 17.
What is the other number?   . . . .   `1` `☐`

> ## TOP TIP!
> Difference means the result you get by subtracting the smallest number from
> the biggest number. Think about the difference in age between you and your
> Maths teacher.

23–24

The difference between two numbers is 19. One of the numbers is 23.

What could the other number be? . . . . or . . . .   `2` `☐`

25   When I take 3 times a certain number from 70 the remainder is 13.

What is the number? . . . .   `1` `☐`

`Total` `☐`
`25`

Measures

Equivalent measures

It is very useful to be able to use and convert between different units of measure. Here are a few of the most frequently used.

1 km = 1000 m	1 m= 100 cm	1 cm = 10 mm
1 tonne = 1000 kg	1 kg = 1000 g	
1 litre = 1	l = 100 cl	
$1 m^2 = 10\ 000\ cm^2$	$1 cm^2 = 100\ mm^2$	
$1 m^2 = 100 \times 100\ cm^2$	$1 cm^2 = 10 \times 10\ mm^2$	

Time

There are 365 days in a year. There are 28 days in February, but every 4 years, if the year is a multiple of 4, there is an extra day in February. When this happens it is called a leap year. There are 31 days in January, March, May, July, August, October and December. April, June, September and November have 30 days. Here's a way to help you remember. Tap each of your knuckles, and the wells in between, while reciting the months of the year. Your knuckles, which are higher up than the wells in between, represent the months with 31 days. The wells in between your knuckles represent the months with 30 days. Just remember that February has 28 days (or 29 in a leap year).

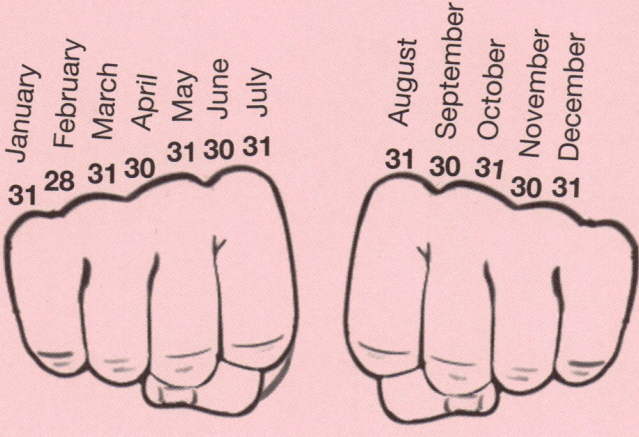

WORKED EXAMPLES

- A room is 5 m long, 3 m wide and 2 m high.

  What is the perimeter of the room, the area of the floor and the volume of the room?

Perimeter	=	distance around the floor	= 5 + 3 + 5 + 3 = **16 m**
Area	=	product of the floor lengths	$= 5 \times 3 =$ **$15 m^2$**
Volume	=	product of all the lengths	$= 5 \times 3 \times 2 =$ **30 m3**

● How much time is there between 10:05 p.m. on Monday and 4:16 a.m. on Wednesday?

You need to know that there are 24 hours in a day, 60 minutes in an hour and 60 seconds in a minute. You also need to know that 9 a.m. is the same as 09:00 in the 24-hour clock and that 9 p.m. is 21:00. The afternoon and evening times are added on to 12 noon.

Change the times in the question to the 24-hour clock: 10:05 p.m. is 22:05 and 4:16 a.m. is 04:16.

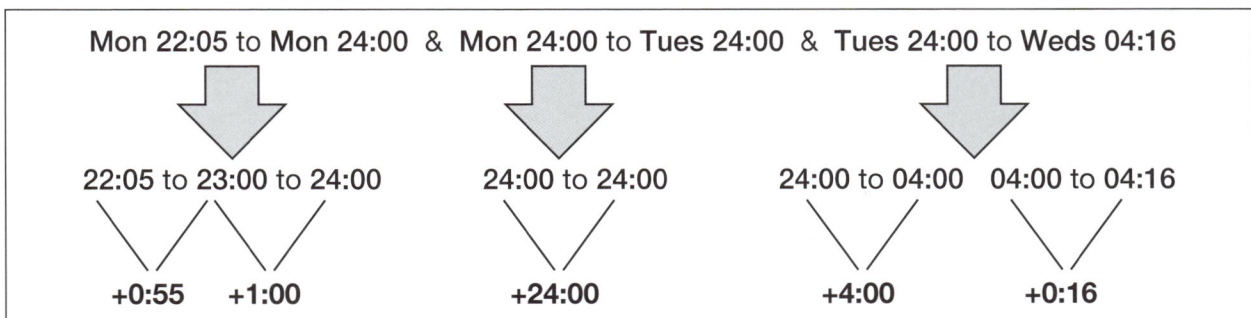

Mon 22:05 to Mon 24:00 & Mon 24:00 to Tues 24:00 & Tues 24:00 to Weds 04:16

22:05 to 23:00 to 24:00   24:00 to 24:00   24:00 to 04:00   04:00 to 04:16

+0:55   +1:00   +24:00   +4:00   +0:16

0:55 + 1:00 + 24:00 + 4:00 + 0:16 = 30:11

30 hrs and 11 minutes

Measures

30 mins

Area

3 m

5 m   1 m

Floor tiles   1 m

1   What is the area of this carpet in m²? ....   `1`

2   How many tiles of size 50 cm × 50 cm will fit in a square size 1 m × 1 m? ....   `1`

3   How many times can you put 2500 cm² into 15 m²? ....   `1`

4–6 Complete the following table.

	Length	Width	Perimeter
Rectangle 1	7 m	5 m	.... m
Rectangle 2	6 m	.... m	20 m
Rectangle 3	.... m	3 m	22 m

`3`

27

Area and Perimeter

7 What is the area of a floor 2.5 m × 3.5 m? 1

8 If the area of a room is 14 m² and the length is 4 m, what is the width? 1

Volume

┌ ─ ┐

TOP TIP!

Always check that the measurements are all in the same unit, and preferably in the same unit as the answer. For example, if you want the area in mm², then convert all the lengths into mm.

└ ─ ┘

9–11

Complete the following table.

	Length	Width	Height	Volume
Cuboid 1	7 cm	5 cm	2 cm	.... cm³
Cuboid 2	8 m	.... m	3 m	96 m³
Cuboid 3	2 mm	1.2 cm	.... mm	120 mm³

3

Length

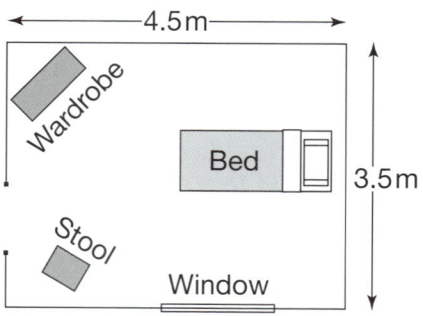

Scale: 1 cm represents 1 m

12–13

My bedroom is .... m long and is .... m wide. 2

14 The window is .... m long. 1

Mass

15 How many 250 g packets of biscuits can be made from 2 kg of biscuits? 1

16 Add together 9 kg, 276 g and 14.5 kg. . . . . kg   `1`

17 Add together 8 kg, 408 g and 1.23 tonnes. Find the answer in kg. . . . . kg   `1`

Capacity

A   B

18 A contains . . . . ml.   `1`

19 B contains . . . . ml.   `1`

20 How much liquid is required to fill jug A up to 1 litre? . . . . ml   `1`

Time

21 How many days are there in the first 3 months of a leap year? . . . .   `1`

We have lessons from 9 o'clock until noon and then from 2 p.m. until 3:30 p.m.
We have two breaks of 15 minutes each in a day.

22 We work . . . . hours a day.   `1`

23 The London train, due to arrive at 11:57 a.m.,
is 14 minutes late. At what time will it arrive? . . . .   `1`

Mixed Measures Questions

Indicate which is larger by writing < or > in each space.

24 4100 m . . . . 4.09 km   `1`

25 999 ml . . . . 1.009 litre   `1`

Total 25

Measures

29

Shape, Space, Position and Direction

KEY SKILLS

2D shape names

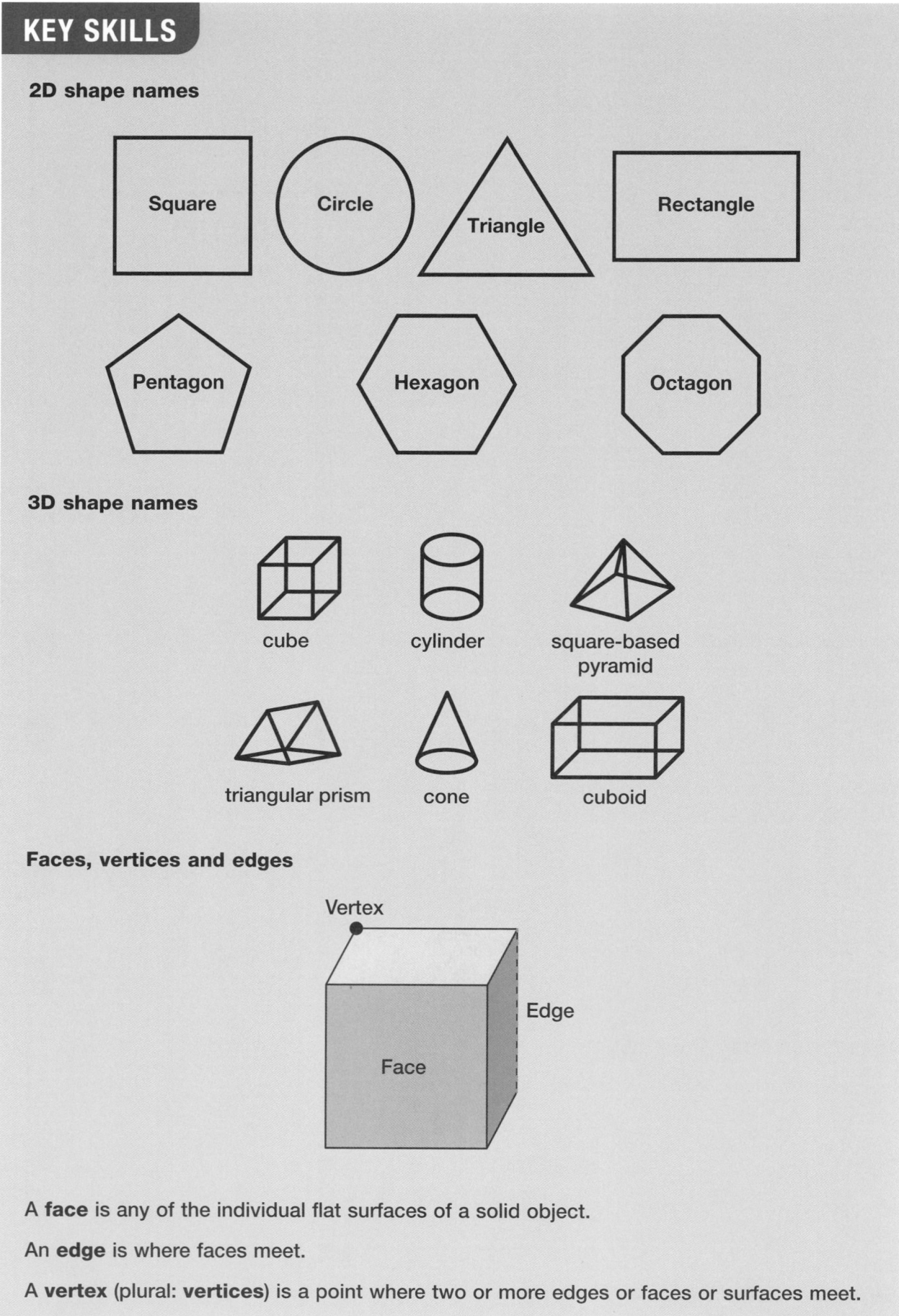

Square

Circle

Triangle

Rectangle

Pentagon

Hexagon

Octagon

3D shape names

cube

cylinder

square-based
pyramid

triangular prism

cone

cuboid

Faces, vertices and edges

Vertex

Edge

Face

A **face** is any of the individual flat surfaces of a solid object.

An **edge** is where faces meet.

A **vertex** (plural: **vertices**) is a point where two or more edges or faces or surfaces meet.

Angle facts and types of angles

Angles on one side of a straight line add up to 180°.

Angles around a point add up to 360°.

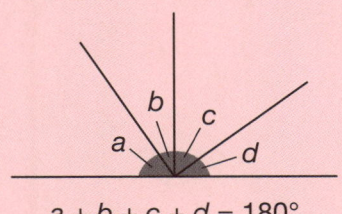

$a + b + c + d = 180°$

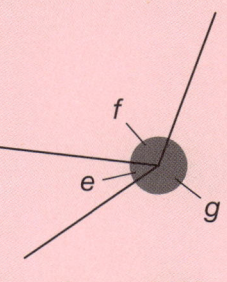

$e + f + g = 360°$

Acute angle

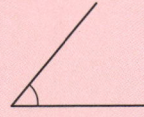

Obtuse angle

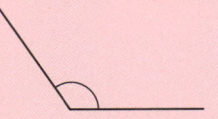

Reflex angle

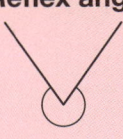

An acute angle is less than 90°, an obtuse angle is more than 90° and a reflex angle is bigger than 180° and less than 360°.

WORKED EXAMPLES

Translate the triangle 5 units to the right. What are the new coordinates for the vertex (1, 1) after the translation?

Reflect the triangle in the mirror line. What are the new coordinates for the vertex (0, 4) after the reflection?

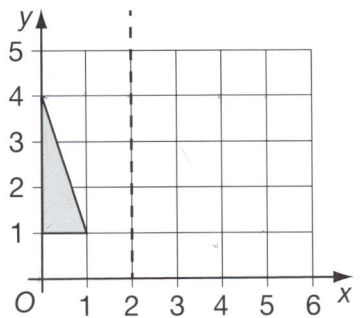

A translation is a slide, every point moves exactly the same amount. The translation point goes to **(6, 1)**.

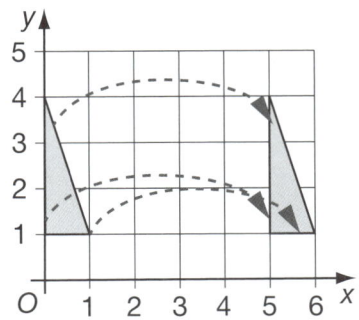

31

With a reflection, the image is reversed and each point on the object is the same distance away from the mirror line as the original image. The reflected point is **(4, 4)**.

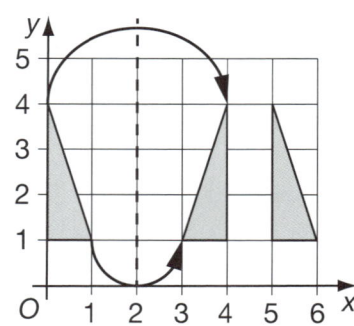

30 mins

2D Shapes

Write the number of pairs of **parallel** sides in each **polygon**.

> **TOP TIP!**
>
> Parallel lines always stay the same distance from each other, they will never meet or cross. The opposite sides of a square are parallel. In real life, imagine train tracks.

1   2 1

2   1 1

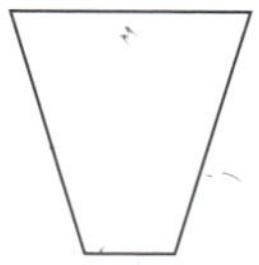

3   4 1

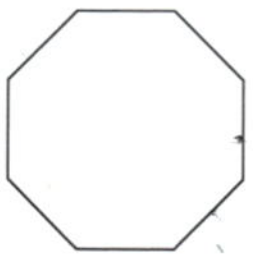

4   0 1

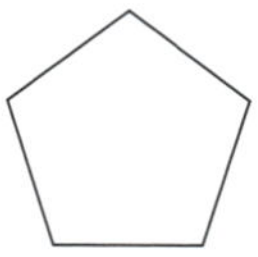

3D Shapes

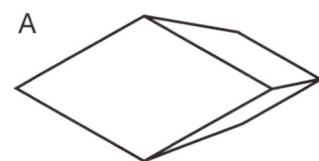
A

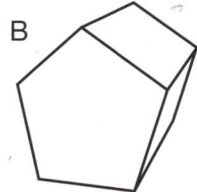
B

5–7

Complete the table.

	A	**B**
Number of **faces**	6	~~7~~
Number of **vertices**		10
Number of **edges**	12	

3

On a Straight Line

8

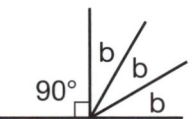
35°
a 90°

Angle a = $180 - 35 + 90 = 55°$

1

9

b b
90° b

Angle b = ...

1

Around a Point

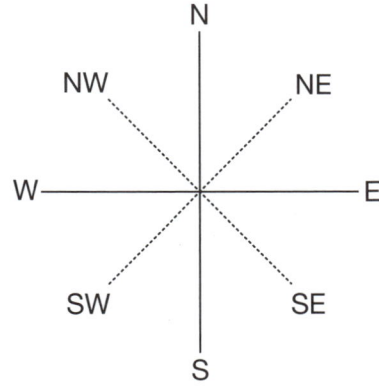

N

NW   NE

W ———————— E

SW   SE

S

10 What is the size of the smaller angle between N and E? ....

1

11 How many degrees are there between N and S? ....

1

12 What is the size of the smaller angle between SE and W? ....

1

Types of Angles

Write whether each angle is **acute, obtuse** or a **right angle**.

13

Acute

.... 1

14

Obtuse

.... 1

15

Right

.... 1

16

Right

.... 1

Symmetry

- -

TOP TIP!

Rotate the book to help you do symmetry. Most people prefer to have a vertical or horizontal line of symmetry. Which do you prefer?

- -

17–20

Circle the polygons that show a correct axis of symmetry.

A   B   C   D

E   F   G   H

4

Coordinates and Transformations

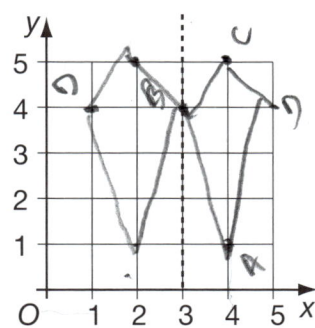

21–24

Plot and label the points A (4, 1), B (3, 4), C (4, 5), D (5, 4). Join up the points.

4

25 Reflect the shape in the mirror line. Draw all the diagonals in the second shape.

How many lines of symmetry does the whole shape have? . . . .1. . . . .

1

Total
25

Statistics

KEY SKILLS

Venn diagrams

Any numbers in an overlap of rings represent people or things that are in both groups. Always look to see if there is a number outside the rectangle which shows the total number inside. Also look for any numbers outside any of the rings as these people do not do any of the activities.

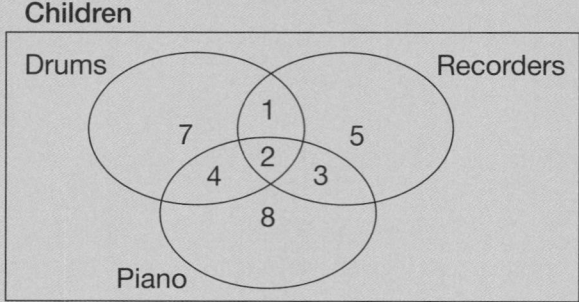

This Venn diagram is about children and instruments; there is no number outside the rectangle to tell us the total. There is no number outside all the rings, which means there is nobody who doesn't play one of these instruments. The 7 tells us there are 7 children who only play the drums. The 1 tells us 1 person plays the drums and the recorder, but not the piano. Keep reading each value until you understand them all.

Bar charts

As with any charts or graphs, always read all the information available before answering any questions, including the title if there is one.

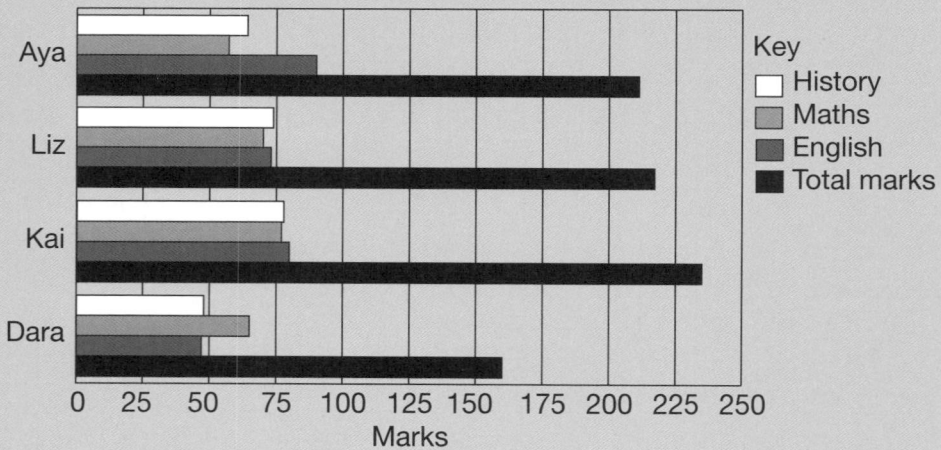

There is no title, but we do know there are 4 people, 3 subjects and a total mark. The scale goes from 0 to 250, each vertical line is an increase of 25 marks. Kai has the biggest total. Dara has the lowest mark of all in English.

Starting from the top: Aya did all 3 subjects, her highest mark was about 82 in English, second was about 65 in History and her lowest was about 60 in Maths. Her total was about 210. Continue doing the same for the other 3 people.

WORKED EXAMPLES

Who had the highest marks in any single exam?

Aya in English. She had about 82 marks compared to Liz who had about 73 marks, Kia who had about 78 marks and Dara who had about 45 marks.

Who had the highest total mark?

Kai. His total mark was about 230.

Who was second in Maths?

Liz. The order was Kai with most marks, then Liz, then Dara then Aya.

Some children were asked which instruments they played. They made this Venn diagram.

Children

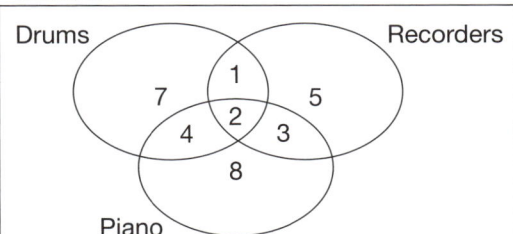

How many children were asked?

How many children play both the piano and the drums?

How many children play the piano or the recorder?

The total is found by adding up all the numbers in all the overlaps and sections which are inside the rectangle. 7 + 1 + 5 + 4 + 2 + 3 + 8 = **30**

Piano AND drums is only those in the overlap. 4 + 2 = **6**

Piano OR the recorder is any inside one or BOTH rings. 1 + 5 + 4 + 2 + 3 + 8 = **23**

30 mins

Venn Diagrams

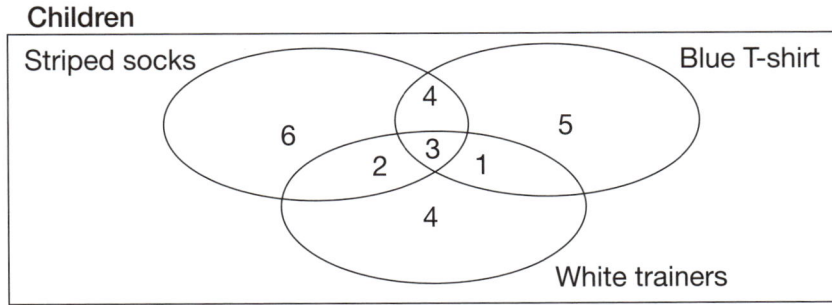

Some children made this Venn diagram to show what they were wearing for PE.

1 How many children were there? .... ⬜ `1`

2 How many wore both blue T-shirts and white trainers? .... ⬜ `1`

3 How many wore blue T-shirts, white trainers and striped socks? .... ⬜ `1`

4 How many wore both white trainers and striped socks but not blue T-shirts?

.... 1

The children in our class made a Venn diagram to show how many had dark hair and brown eyes.

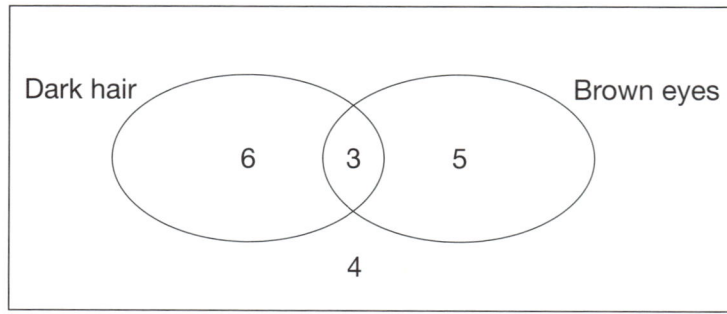

Our class

Dark hair — 6 — 3 — 5 — Brown eyes

4

5 How many children are in our class? 1

6 How many children have dark hair? 1

7 How many have brown eyes? 1

8 How many have both dark hair and brown eyes? 1

9 .... children don't have dark hair. 1

Bar Charts

Here is a bar chart that shows the approximate number of people in Southwich who watch television each night.

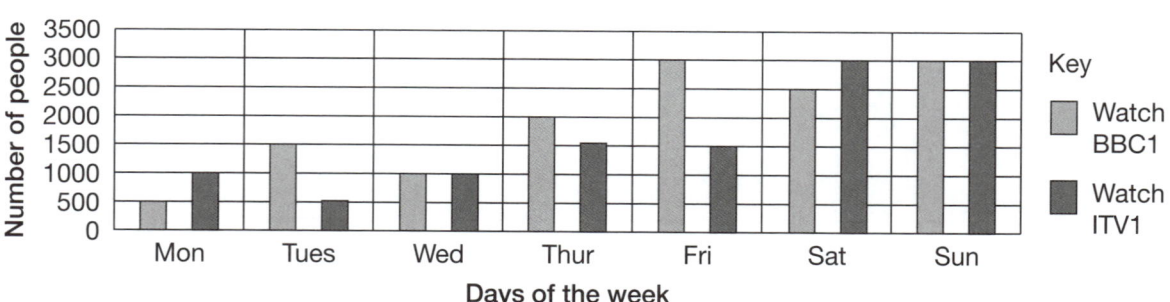

Key

Watch BBC1

Watch ITV1

10–11

On which 2 nights do the same number of people watch BBC1 and ITV1?

.... and 2

12 On which night is there the biggest difference in the number of people who watch

BBC1 and ITV1? .... `1`

13 BBC1 has the fewest viewers on .... `1`

14 ITV1 has the fewest viewers on .... `1`

Line Graphs

Here is a line graph that shows the amount of snow in one week.

TOP TIP!

To read the line graph, either you can slide along the horizontal axis to a particular point first and then straight up to the dark circle, or you can slide up the vertical axis first to a particular point then straight across to the dark circle.

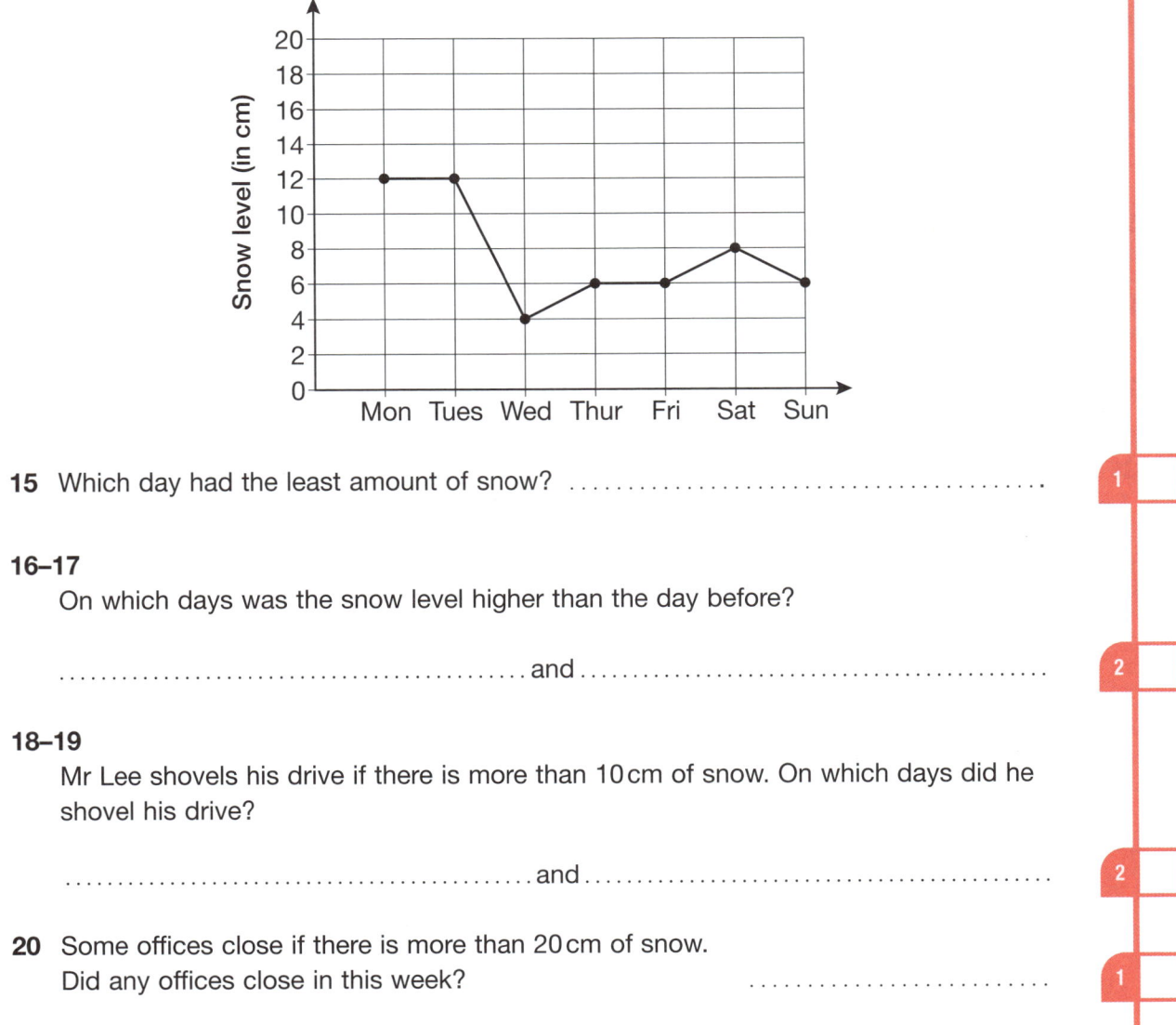

15 Which day had the least amount of snow? .... `1`

16–17

On which days was the snow level higher than the day before?

.... and .... `2`

18–19

Mr Lee shovels his drive if there is more than 10 cm of snow. On which days did he shovel his drive?

.... and .... `2`

20 Some offices close if there is more than 20 cm of snow.
Did any offices close in this week? .... `1`

Pictograms

Learning Papers

Statistics

> **TOP TIP!**
>
> Always check the key on pictograms and work out what half of one of the pictures represents. In this question it would represent half a child, which would not make sense! But pictograms often use half of the key image.

The children in Class 4 drew this pictogram to show where they live.

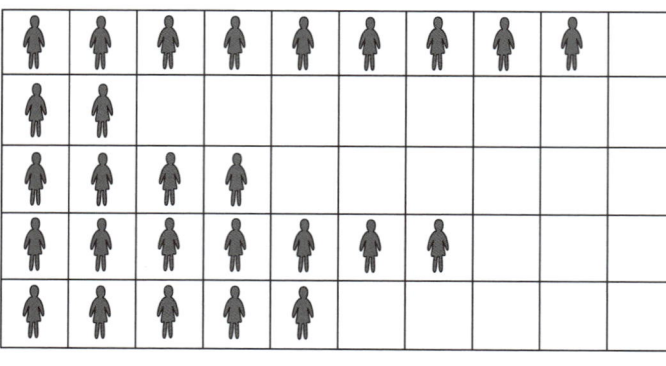

	Key
	♟ represents one child

21 How many children live in High Street? .... **1** ☐

22 How many children live in Abbey Crescent? .... **1** ☐

23 How many children live in Shore Drive? .... **1** ☐

24 How many more children live in Low Road than in Bay Avenue? .... **1** ☐

25 What fraction of the class lives in High Street? .... **1** ☐

Total
25 ☐

Word and Logic Problems

KEY SKILLS

With word and logic problems you want to think of a strategy to solve them.

First look for clues, look for relationships and prioritise your steps.

Key words to look for include sum, total, double, halve, add, etc.

Have a look at the following steps and decide which ones will help (you don't need to use all of them).

1 What do I have to find out?

2 How many pieces of information do I have?

3 Which is the most important?

4 Could I solve the problem if I took one piece of information away?

5 Do I need to prioritise the information to solve a problem?

6 Which information can I use first?

7 Where shall I start?

8 Do I just start at the top and work my way down, or do I start at the bottom and work up? Why/why not?

9 Which clue can I use next?

10 Ask questions such as; 'If this … then this will change …', 'What if …?'

11 How am I going to solve the problem, including how recording might help me.

12 Review my work: Where am I? Where do I need to be? Is this working?

13 Does my answer meet all the criteria?

WORKED EXAMPLES

- Find the length of a queue of 21 cars (each car is 4 m long). There is a 1 m space after each of the first 20 cars.

  Try sketching a picture, or place the information in the order it applies.

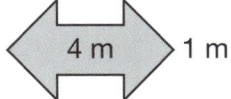 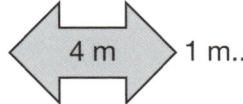 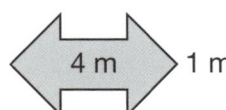 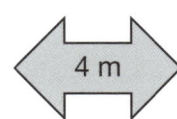

(4 + 1) + (4 + 1) + (4 + 1) + … + (4 + 1) + 4

So we have 21 cars and 20 spaces: 21 × 4 = 84

20 × 1 = 20

And then: 84 + 20 = **104**

• In 4 years' time, Wilf will be half as old as his dad. Wilf's dad is 33 next year.

How old is Wilf now?

We know that Wilf's dad is 33 next year, so he is 32 now.

In 4 years' time, Wilf's dad will be 36.

In 4 years' time, Wilf will be half as old as his dad: 36 ÷ 2 = 18

Wilf is now 18 − 4 = **14**

30 mins

Word Problems

A library charges a fine of 40 pence for each week a book is late.

1   What is the fine if a book is 3 weeks late? **1**

2   What is the fine if 3 books are 4 weeks late? **1**

3   What is the fine if 1 book is 5 weeks late and 2 other books are 6 weeks late?

   .... **1**

£1 = 1.65 US dollars
£1 = 1.2 euros
£1 = 190 Sri Lankan rupees

4   How many US dollars do you get for £100? $ **1**

5   How many Sri Lankan rupees do you get for £50? .... rupees **1**

6   How many euros do you get for £30? € **1**

7   How many pounds do you get for 380 Sri Lankan rupees? £ **1**

£1 = 1.53 US dollars
£1 = 121 Kenyan shillings
£1 = 1.23 euros
£1 = 1.72 Australian dollars

8   How many US dollars do you get for £200? $ **1**

9 How many Kenyan shillings do you get for £5? . . . . shillings

10 How many pounds do you get for 172 Australian dollars? £ . . . .

11 If Phil can swim 15 m in 20 seconds, how far can he swim, at the same speed, in 2 minutes?

. . . .

12 If it takes Maria a quarter of an hour to walk to school, what time must she leave home to get to school by 8:50 a.m.?

. . . .

13 How many books, each 1.2 cm thick, can be stood on a shelf 50.4 cm wide?

. . . .

Logic Problems

14 Underline the amounts below which you can make with these five coins.

19p	28p	33p	29p	37p

- -

TOP TIP!
To find the mean average of two values, add them, then divide by 2.

- -

What number is halfway between:

15 20 and 30? . . . .

16 21 and 35? . . . .

17 17 and 29? . . . .

1
1
1
1
1
1
1
1
1

18 What is the smallest number which must be added to 368 to make it exactly divisible by 27?

.... `1` ☐

19 How many squares 5 cm × 5 cm can I cut from a card 20 cm × 40 cm? .... `1` ☐

There are 28 in our class. One day there were 6 times as many present as there were absent.

20 How many were present? .... `1` ☐

21 How many were absent? .... `1` ☐

22 Kim has 75p and Michael has 91p. How much must Michael give Kim so that they will both have the same amount?

.... `1` ☐

23 How much will each of them have then? .... `1` ☐

The sum of two numbers is 26 and their difference is 8.

24 What is the larger number? .... `1` ☐

25 The smaller number is .... `1` ☐

Total
25 ☐

44

Curveball Questions 1

1   To open the safe you have to replace the question mark with the correct digit.

The numbers are not arranged randomly.

Look for the pattern to work out the missing digits.

First number: . . . .   Second number: 2

. . . .

TOP TIP!

When you are looking for a pattern, look left to right as well as top to bottom.

2   How many different ways are there to choose one dog with pointy ears and one with floppy black ears?

. . . . ways   3

Total
5

Mixed Papers

Mixed Paper 1

50 mins

1–5

Reflect these figures in the lines of symmetry.

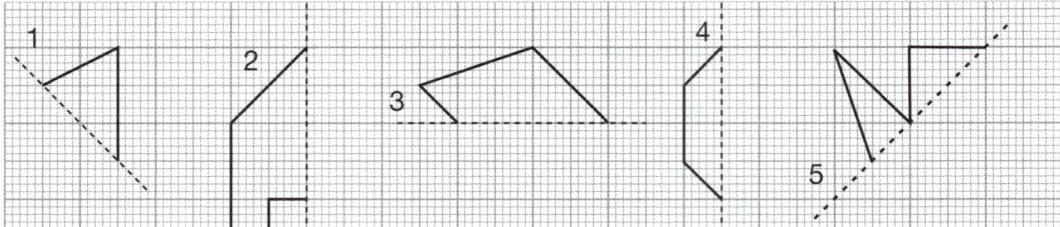

6 Which number multiplied by itself gives 64? **1**

Circle the correct answer for this question.

7 $\dfrac{1}{2} + \dfrac{1}{4} =$ $\dfrac{3}{4}$ $\dfrac{2}{6}$ $\dfrac{1}{6}$ $\dfrac{1}{2}$ **1**

8 What number when divided by 6 has an answer of 7 remainder 3? **1**

9 Divide 28 metres into 8 equal pieces. How long is each piece? **1**

10 What is the biggest number you can make with these digits?   3 2 0 4 6 8

.... **1**

11 Write the answer to question 10 in words. **1**

How many halves do the following contain?

12 $7\dfrac{1}{2}$ **1**

13 $10\dfrac{1}{2}$ **1**

14 23   .... **1**

5

15 How many glasses, each holding $\frac{1}{4}$ litre, could be filled from a bottle holding 2.5 litres?

.... 1

I went to bed at 7:30 p.m. and got up at 7:15 a.m. the next day.

16 How long was I in bed?   ....h...............min   1

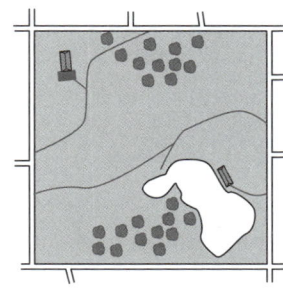

17 What is the area of a square park whose sides are 3 km?
Choose the correct units from: cm, cm², m, m², m³, km, km².   1

18 What is the perimeter of the park? 1

19 If the area of another square park is 16 km², what is the length of one side?
Choose the correct units from: cm, cm², m, m², m³, km, km².   1

20 What is the perimeter of this park? 1

Fill in the missing figures.

21   5 minutes × .... = 1 hour   1

22   20 cm × .... = 1 metre   1

23   125 ml × .... = 1 litre   1

24   50 m × .... = 1 km   1

25
$$\begin{array}{r} 78.05 \\ 9.92 \\ +\ \ 5.07 \\ \hline \\ \hline \end{array}$$

1

26 What is the perimeter of a rectangle with length 9.5 cm and width 13 cm?

.... cm

1

I gave Tanya half of my chocolates and was left with 37.

27 How many did I have to start with? ....

1

28   9.420
      − 7.860
      _____

      _____

1

29 If $\frac{3}{5}$ of my money is 21p, how much do I have? ....

1

30 Twice a number is 36. What is three times the number? ....

1

31 Laura ate four-fifths of her sweets. If she had 6 left, how many sweets did she have to start with?

....

1

TOP TIP!

Km/h mean kilometres per hour. If you are travelling at 60 km/h, you will travel 60 km in 1 hour, which is the same as 1 km per minute.

32 How long will it take a lorry to go 325 km
at a constant speed of 50 km/h?   .... h .... min

1

33 Take 22 cm from 13 m.   .... m

1

Our class made this bar chart, which shows our favourite pets.

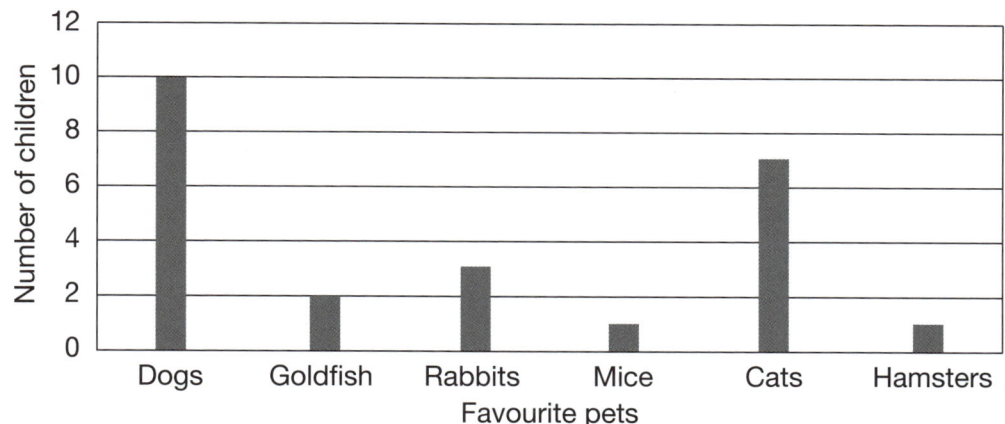

34 How many children are there in our class? ....

35 What fraction of the class prefers rabbits? 1

36 How many children prefer dogs? 1

37 How many children like hamsters best? 1

38 How many more children like dogs than like cats? 1

Write each fraction as a decimal.

39 $\dfrac{22}{100}$  1

40 $\dfrac{22}{50}$ 1

Total **40**

Mixed Paper 2

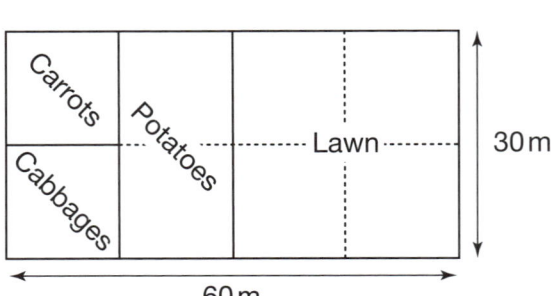

50 mins

1 What percentage of the garden is lawn? .... % ▪1▫

2 What fraction of the garden is for cabbages? .... ▪1▫

3 What percentage of the garden is for potatoes? .... % ▪1▫

4 What fraction of the garden is for carrots? .... ▪1▫

5 What is the area of the garden? .... m² ▪1▫

6 What is the area of the lawn? .... m² ▪1▫

7 What is three squared? .... ▪1▫

8 10 minutes × .... = 1 hour ▪1▫

Circle the correct answer for this question.

9 What is $\frac{1}{2}$ of 7?   14 $\frac{2}{5}$ $3\frac{1}{2}$ $6\frac{1}{2}$ ▪1▫

10 If my car uses 1 litre of petrol every 10 km, how many litres will I need to drive 105 km?

....

11 There are 3 boys for every 2 girls in a class of 25 children. How many girls are there?

.... ▪1▫

12–14

Plot and label the points A (1, 0), B (2, 3), C (3, 0).

Join up the points.

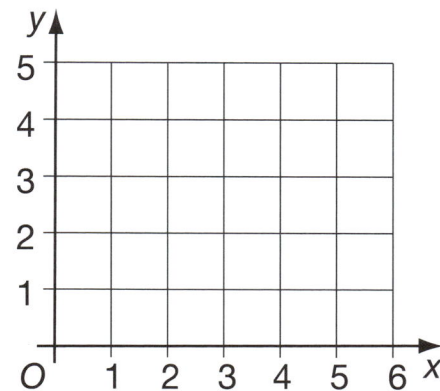

3

15 What is the name of this shape? 1

16 How many lines of symmetry does it have? 1

17 Translate the shape 2 units to the right. Draw the new position. 1

Look at the letters below. They form a pattern.

18 a b c d e a b c d e . . . What would the eighteenth letter be? 1

19 x y z x y z . . . What would the tenth letter be? 1

20 Add together $\frac{1}{8}$ and $\frac{1}{2}$ 1

| 51 | 67 | 80 | 91 | 143 |

Which of the numbers in the box:

21 is divisible by 7? 1

22 is divisible by 3? 1

23 is divisible by 11? 1

24 What is $6^2 - 3^2$? 1

25 My alarm clock loses a minute a day. If I put it right at noon on Monday, what time will it show at noon on Thursday?

.... `1` ☐

Using all of the digits 5, 2, 6, 3 and 1 once only, make:

26 the smallest number. .... `1` ☐

27 the smallest odd number. .... `1` ☐

28 the largest number. .... `1` ☐

29 the largest even number. .... `1` ☐

Indicate which is larger by writing < or > in each space.

30 5.001 m .... 5.01 m `1` ☐

31 6.99 km .... 6.099 km `1` ☐

32 We bought 120 cakes for a party, 27 were left. How many were eaten? .... `1` ☐

33 By how much is 3.5 greater than 0.6? .... `1` ☐

34 Take 347 centimetres from 5.2 metres .... cm `1` ☐

35

```
   87
   65
   46
   38
+  25
_____
```

Here is a pictogram which shows how many people went to the Cyber Café last week.
Use it to answer the questions.

Mon	𝄖	𝄖	𝄖	𝄖	⌇	
Tues	𝄖	𝄖	𝄖	𝄖	𝄖	⌇
Wed	𝄖	𝄖	⌇			
Thur	𝄖	𝄖	𝄖	𝄖	𝄖	𝄖
Fri	𝄖	𝄖	𝄖	𝄖	𝄖	𝄖
Sat	𝄖	𝄖	𝄖	𝄖	𝄖	⌇

Key

𝄖 = 50 people

36 How many people visited on Friday? ....

37 How many people visited on Tuesday? ....

38 How many more people went to the café on Thursday than Wednesday? ....

Fill in the missing numbers.

39 6 × 7 × .... = 420

40 2 × 3 × .... = 300

1

1

1

1

1

1

Total
40

Mixed Paper 3

50 mins

What fraction of each shape is shaded or dotted?

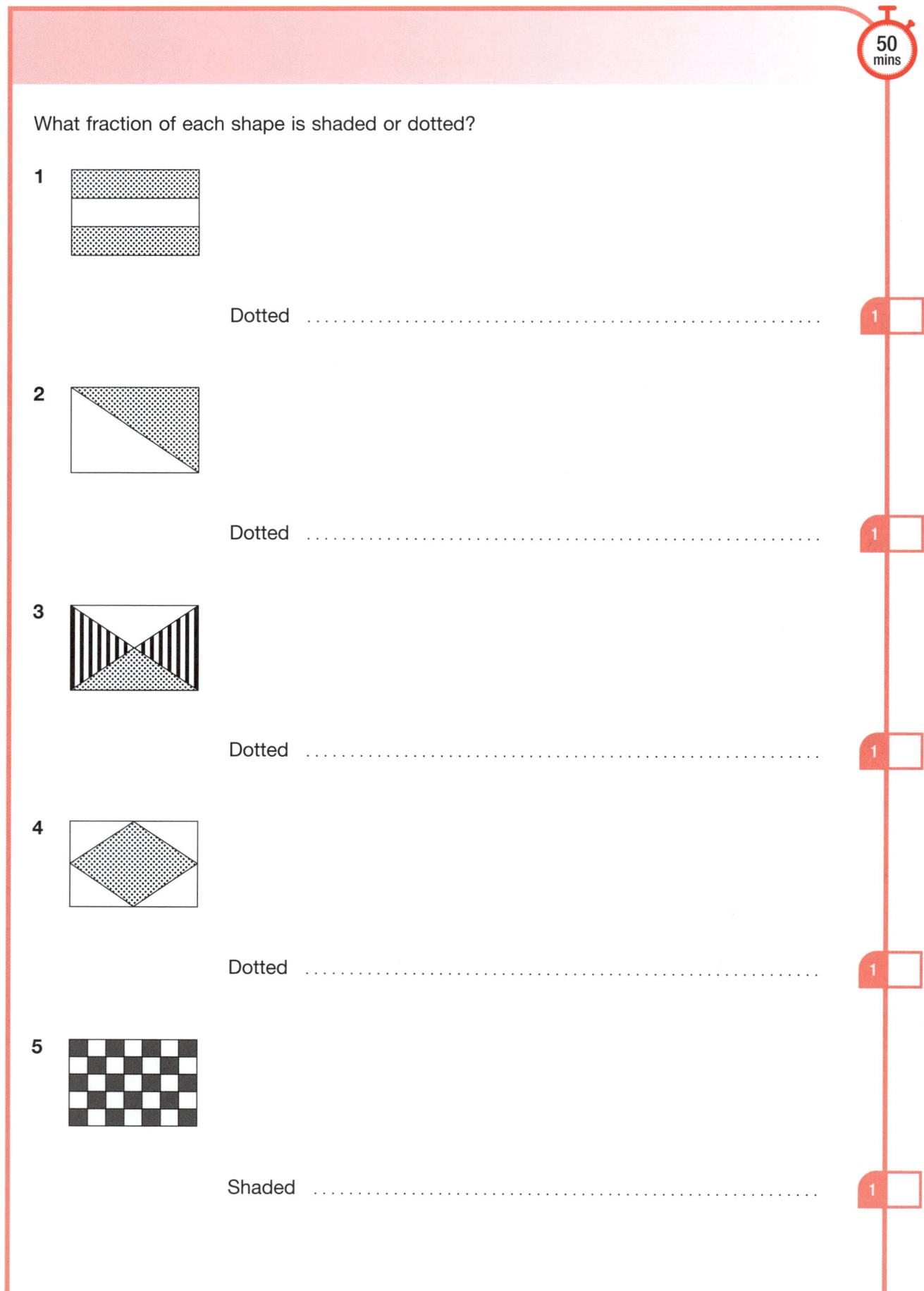

1

Dotted 1

2

Dotted 1

3

Dotted 1

4

Dotted 1

5

Shaded 1

In a school of 300 children $\frac{3}{5}$ are boys.

6 How many boys are there? .... `1`

7 How many girls are there? .... `1`

Paul and Meena each have a piece of string. Paul's piece is 6.70 m long and Meena's is 5.84 m.

8 Who has the longer piece? .... `1`

9 How many centimetres longer is it? .... `1`

10 What is 7583 to the nearest 1000? .... `1`

11–13

The distance from London to Jeddah is 5904 miles. This is approximately ....

miles to the nearest 1000 miles, ... miles to the nearest 100 miles and

.... miles to the nearest 10 miles. `3`

Use these two calculations to help you answer the following questions.

$$\begin{array}{r} 712 \\ -\ 368 \\ \hline 344 \end{array} \qquad \begin{array}{r} 357 \\ +\ 345 \\ \hline 702 \end{array}$$

14 368 + 344 = ... `1`

15 702 – 345 = ... `1`

16 712 – 368 = ... `1`

17 702 – 357 = ... `1`

18 712 – 344 = ... `1`

19–22

Complete this multiplication table.

×				
	56	42		77
		48	32	88
	72		36	

4

23 If the distance all round a square is 24 cm, what is the length of each side?

.... cm

1

Wobbly Custard Powder can be bought in three sizes.

A 500 g tin costs £1.85, a 250 g tin costs 99p and a 125 g tin costs 54p.

24 What would you save if you bought one 250 g tin instead of two 125 g tins?

£ ....

1

25 How much cheaper is it to buy a 500 g tin than four 125 g tins?   £ ....

1

School starts at 8:55 a.m. One day Katie was quarter of an hour late.

26 What time did she arrive?   ....

1

Write the next two numbers in each of the following lines.

27–28

    8   4   2   1   ....

2

29–30

    1.25   1.50   1.75   ....

2

There are 30 children in Class 4. There are 2 girls to every 3 boys.

31–32

There are .... girls and .... boys in Class 4.

33
$$
\begin{array}{r}
9191 \\
-\ 1717 \\
\hline
\end{array}
$$

TOP TIP!

BIDMAS – brackets before indices, before divide, before multiply, before add, before subtract. Indices is the same as powers or order.

What is:

34 $6^2 + 11^2$? ....

35 $9^2 + 2^2$? ....

36 $8^2 + 12^2$? ....

37 If you use a quarter of a 25 kg bag of cement, how may grammes are left? ...... g

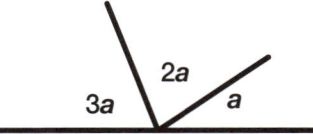

38 Angle a = ...°

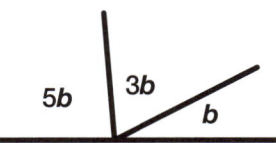

39 Angle b = ...°

40 Find the volume of a cube in m³. Each side is 200 cm long. .... m³

Total 40

Mixed Paper 4

50 mins

1 The pairs of factors of 15 are: 1 and 15, 3 and ....

1

2–3

The pairs of factors of 12 are: 1 and ...., 2 and ...., 3 and 4.

2

Circle the correct answer.

4 How many $\frac{1}{2}$ in 2?　　　　$\frac{1}{2}$　　　1　　　2　　　4

1

5 Angle c = ...

1

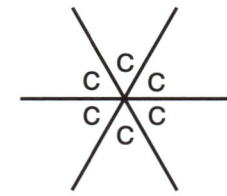

Write TRUE or FALSE for the following:

6 (245 × 10) > (24 × 100)　　　　..

1

7 (2.45 × 100) < (24 × 10)　　　　..

1

8 (24.5 × 10) < (2.4 × 100)　　　　..

1

9 (0.245 × 100) > (24 × 10)　　　　..

1

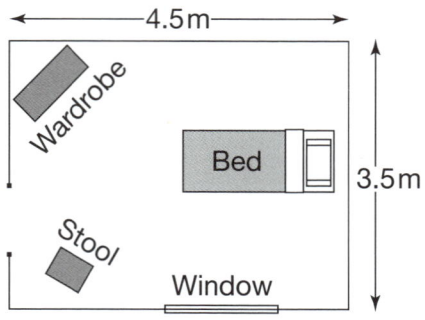

Scale: 1 cm represents 1 m

10 The bed is .... m long.

1

58

11 The wardrobe is . . . . m long. `1`

12 The stool is . . . . m long. `1`

> ### TOP TIP!
> There are 8 pints in a gallon. 1 pint = 568 ml

What is the best approximation for a gallon? Underline your choice.

13 1 litre   2 litres   3 litres   4 litres   5 litres   6 litres `1`

14 What number is 12 more than 19? . . . . `1`

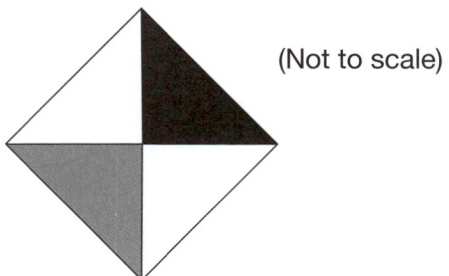

(Not to scale)

15 What is the area of this square? Each side is 4 cm. . . . . `1`

16 What is the area of the grey part? . . . . `1`

17 What is the total area of the white parts? . . . . `1`

18–20

There are 96 roses in a bed in the park. 50% of them are yellow, $\frac{1}{4}$ are red, and the rest are pink.

. . . . roses are red, ... are yellow and . . . . are pink. `3`

21–22

Jasmina and Sharon shared 24 book tokens.

Jasmina had 2 more than Sharon, so she had . . . .

and Sharon had . . . . `2`

Here is a bar chart showing the highest temperature in seven cities last winter.

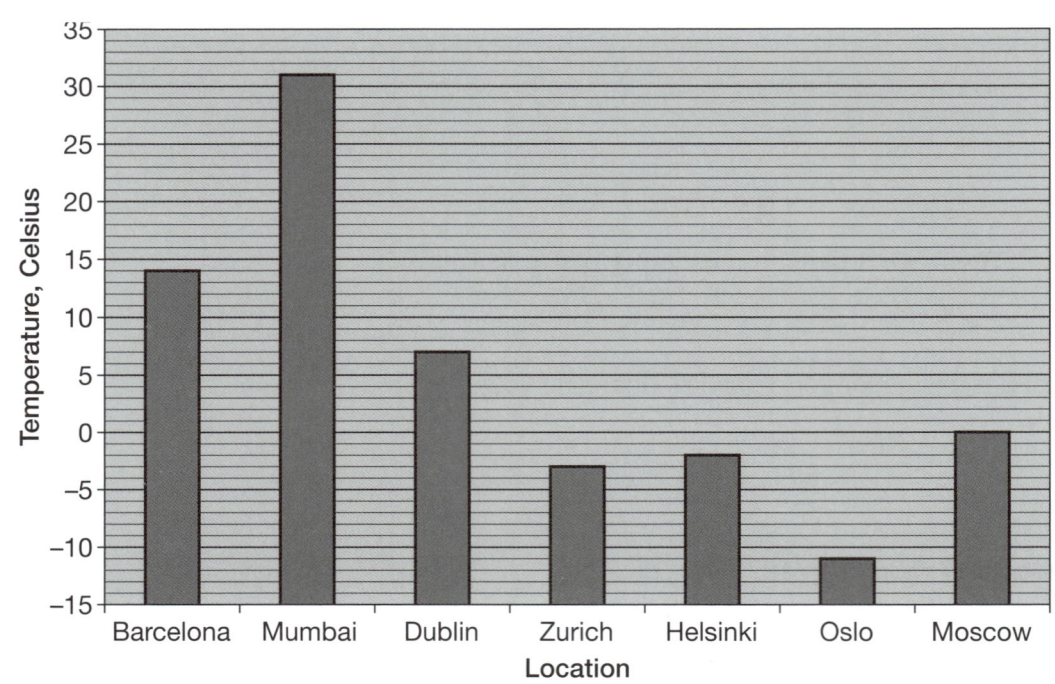

Find the difference in temperature between:

23 Mumbai and Dublin. ....°C 1

24 Zurich and Barcelona. ....°C 1

25 Moscow and Zurich. ....°C 1

26 Helsinki and Oslo. ....°C 1

27 How many days are there in spring (March, April and May)? 1

Fill in the missing numbers.

28 $3 \times 0.007 =$ 1

29 $4 \times 10.1 =$ 1

The sum of two numbers is 31.

30 If one number is 15, what is the other number? 1

A cranberry juice concentrate needs 5 parts of water to every 1 part of concentrate.

31 How many litres of juice can you make with $\frac{1}{2}$ litre of concentrate? . . . .

A piece of rope 2.34 m long is cut into 9 equal pieces.

32 How long is each piece? Give your answer in centimetres. . . . .

33 Add $\frac{1}{4}$ of 48 to twice 19. . . . .

34 Take one hundred and seventy-seven from ten thousand. 1

Our class made this Venn diagram to show how many children like art best and how many like PE best.

Our class

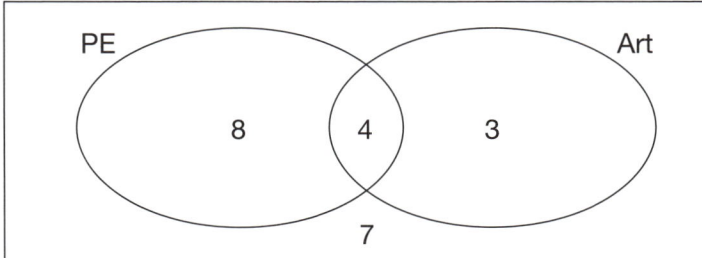

35 How many are in our class? . . . .

36–37

. . . . like PE and . . . . like art. 2

38 How many children like both art and PE? . . . .

39–40

. . . . children don't like PE and . . . . don't like art. 2

Total
40

Curveball Questions 2

20 mins

1 All the numbers fit on the triangle so that the sum of the numbers on each side are equal.

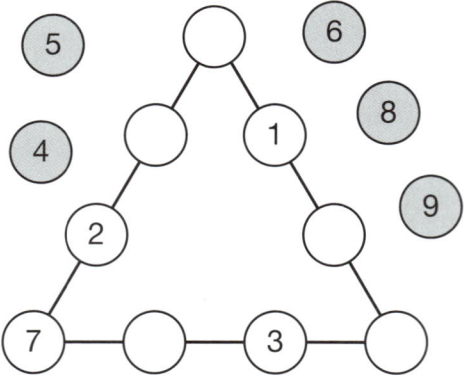

Some of the numbers have already been placed for you, these cannot change position.

What is the total of each side?

Side total = ...

5

2 How many different ways are there to choose three red fruit or vegetables and one yellow fruit or vegetable?

. . . . ways

1

Total 6

Test Papers

Test Paper 1

60 mins

TOP TIP!

Before you start the test paper make sure you have enough time available to complete it. When you start, the first thing to do is to look through all the questions so you know how long the paper is and check what the last page looks like. If you finish early, go back and check your answers.

1–6

Put a ring around the shapes that are regular polygons.

6

A train left Dover at 11:25 a.m. and arrived in London at 13:03.

7 How long did the journey take? .... h.......... min **1**

8 What fraction of the large square is covered with dots? **1**

9 What fraction, in lowest terms, is grey? **1**

10 What fraction, in lowest terms, is white? **1**

63

11 What is the area of the whole large square? .... `1`

12 What is the total area of the grey squares? .... `1`

13 What is the total area of the white squares? .... `1`

14 What size is the smaller angle between 12 and 3? .... `1`

15 What size is the smaller angle between 2 and 3? .... `1`

16 The smaller angle between 4 and 6 is .... `1`

17 The smaller angle between 6 and 9 is .... `1`

18 The angle between 6 and 12 is .... `1`

19 The smaller angle between 7 and 8 is .... `1`

20 $2000 - 2 =$ .... `1`

21 $350 + 63 =$ .... `1`

22 $1990 + 20 =$ .... `1`

23 What is the smallest number you can make by arranging these digits?

3, 5, 4, 9, 3, 4 .... `1`

24 Write the answer to question 23 in words. ....

.... `1`

25 I went to the cinema at 2:55 p.m. and came out at 5:35 p.m.
How long was I there? ....h..........min `1`

Fill in the missing numbers.

26

$$8\overline{)}^{\text{7 rem 3}}$$

1 ....

27

$$9\overline{)}^{\text{5 rem 4}}$$

.... 1

28

$$7\overline{)38}^{\underline{}\text{ rem 3}}$$

.... 1

29

$$9\overline{)39}^{\underline{}\text{ rem 3}}$$

.... 1

30–33

Reflect these shapes in the mirror lines.

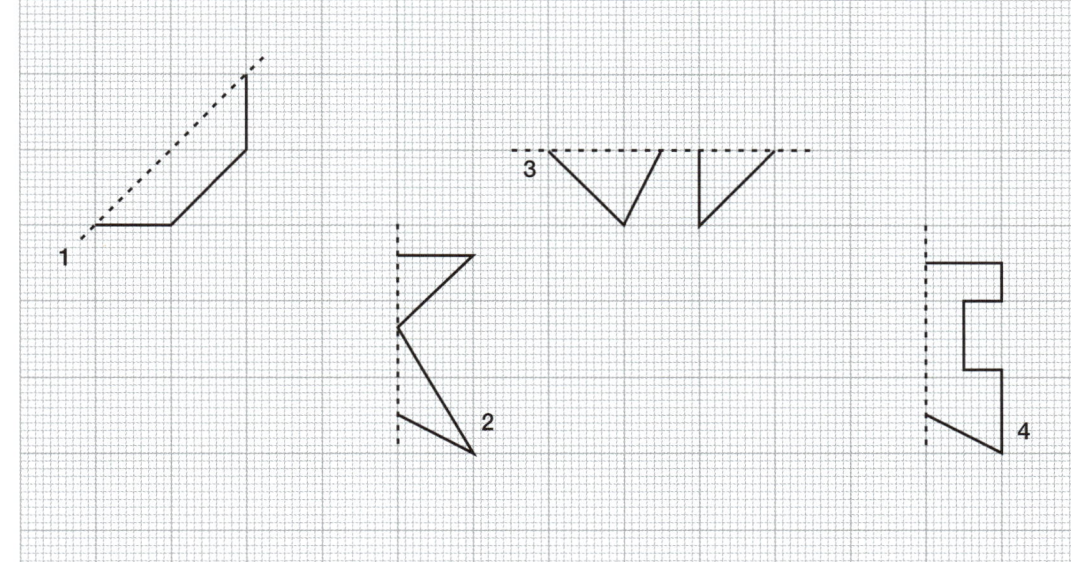

3

34 Multiply 20 by itself. 1

35 Which number, when multiplied by itself, gives 169? 1

Give each answer as a mixed number in the lowest terms.

36 $3 - 1\frac{9}{10} =$ 1

37 $5 - 2\frac{1}{7} =$ 1

38 The distance all round a square is 3.4 m. How long is each side in centimetres?

.... 1

39
```
   7.69
   4.82
 + 3.68
 _____

 _____
```
1

Here is a bar chart to show the number of people who came to see our school play.

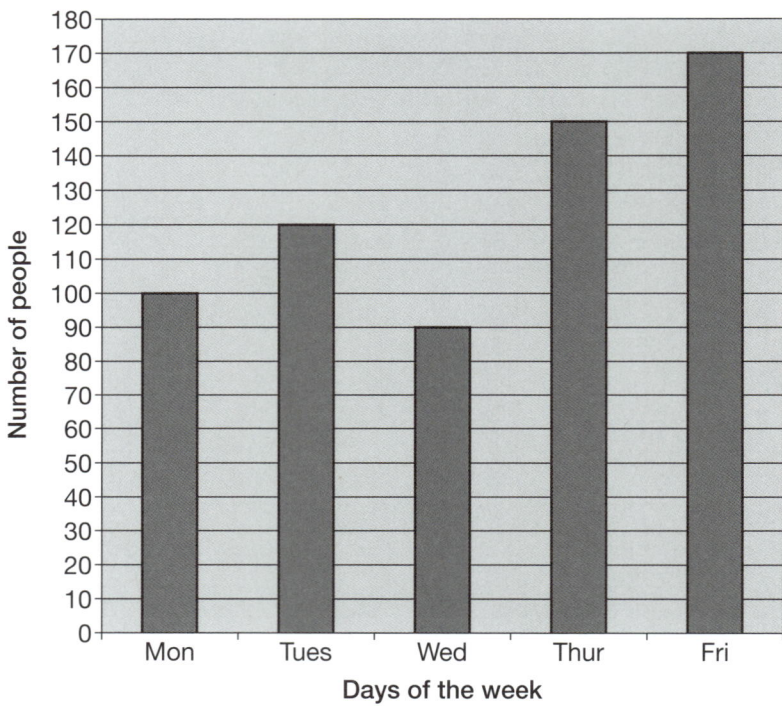

40 How many people came on Monday? 1

41 How many people came on Wednesday? 1

42 What was the least popular day? 1

43 The total audience was 1

44 What is the area of a square of length 11 cm? ....cm² 1

45 If there are 20 lines on each page, on which page will the one hundred and tenth line appear? 1

46 Rob had 52 battle game cards. He lost 16, then won back twice as many as he had lost. 1

How many has he got now? ....

47 345 × 300 = ... 1

Write the following decimals as fractions in their lowest terms.

48 0.4 1

49 0.25 1

50 0.9 1

51 0.03 1

52 0.01 1

53 0.07 1

54–57

The pairs of factors of 27 are:

.... , ... and .... , ... 4

Complete these questions by filling in the missing numbers.

58 $\dfrac{}{7} = \dfrac{8}{28}$ 1

59 $\dfrac{}{9} = \dfrac{20}{36}$ 1

60 $\dfrac{8}{9} = \dfrac{}{54}$ 1

Here is a chart that shows the height in centimetres of each of my friends.

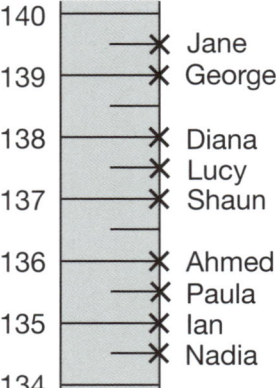

61 How much taller is Jane than Lucy? .... `1`

62 How much taller is George than Paula? .... `1`

63 How much shorter is Ian than Lucy? .... `1`

64 What is the difference in height between Shaun and Nadia? .... `1`

65–66

In a school there are 200 pupils. $\frac{2}{5}$ of them are girls. There are girls and boys.

How many girls are there and how many boys are there?

.... girls .... boys `2`

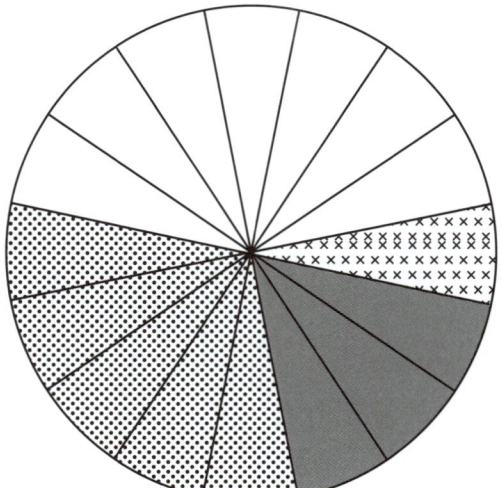

What fraction of the circle is each of
the following? (Remember to express
fractions in the lowest terms)

67 Dotted .... `1`

68 Grey ....

69–70

What fraction of the circle is dotted and grey? 1

71 An orange juice concentrate needs 4 parts of water to every
1 part of concentrate. How many litres of juice can you make
with 0.6 litres of concentrate? 1

72 The train due at 10:53 was 11 minutes late. When did it arrive? 1

73–76

Arrange these decimals in order, putting the largest first.

| 2.02 | 2.2 | 2.222 | 2.22 |

....   4

77 Take 11 from eleven thousand. 1

78 My sourdough bread mixture uses 300 ml of water,
half a kg of flour, 200 g of starter and 2 g of salt for
one loaf. Assuming 1 ml of water weighs 1 g,
what is the total weight of 3 loaves? .... kg   1

79–80

A cuboid has the same width and height. The length is triple the width.

If the volume is 192 cm³, find the width and the length.

Width = ... cm, length = ... cm.   2

Total
80

Test Paper 2

60 mins

TOP TIP!

Make sure you are not going to get distracted, find a quiet place and get everything you need before you start the test. If you are not told to do each question in order, skip through, choosing some of your favourite questions first.

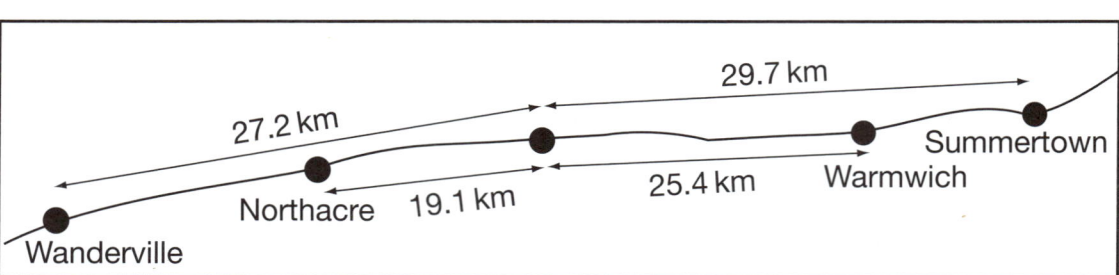

29.7 km

27.2 km

Summertown

Warmwich

Northacre   19.1 km   25.4 km

Wanderville

1   How far is it from Northacre to Summertown? .... km   1

2   How far is it from Wanderville to Summertown? .... km   1

3   How far is it from Warmwich to Northacre? .... km   1

4   How far is it from Warmwich to Wanderville? .... km   1

5   Multiply 4 by itself.   1

6   What is 7^2?   1

7   How many times can I take 8 from 200?   1

8   Take the product of 6 and 7 from 50.   1

What is the best approximation for a mile? Underline your choice.

9   0.5 km   1 km   1.5 km   2 km   2.5 km   1

70

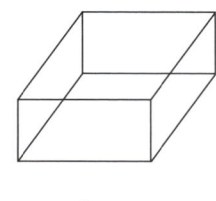

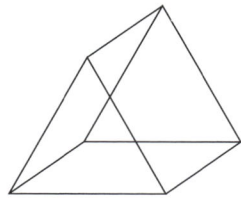

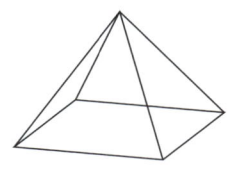

A   **B**   **C**

10–18

Complete the table.

	A	**B**	**C**
Number of **faces**			
Number of **vertices**			
Number of **edges**			

`9`

19 $\frac{24}{100} + \frac{13}{100} - \frac{8}{100} =$ ....

`1`

20 478 + 199 = 677 ....

`1`

If I took 100 away from both numbers (478 and 199), the answer would be:

the same   200 less   100 more

21 478 − 199 = 279 ....

`1`

If I took 100 away from both numbers (478 and 199), the answer would be:

the same   200 less   100 more

22 How many quarters are there in $7\frac{3}{4}$? ....

`1`

23 Multiply 47 by 200. ....

`1`

24 How many minutes are there between noon and 13:29? ....

`1`

25 How many weeks are there in 266 days? ....

`1`

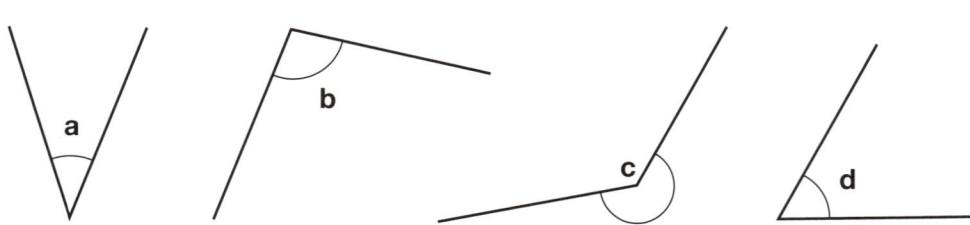

Using the words acute, obtuse or **reflex,** describe the above angles. Use a protractor to find the size of the angles to the nearest 1°.

26–27

a is............................., and is approximately.............................°.   `2`

28–29

b is............................., and is approximately.............................°.   `2`

30–31

c is............., and is approximately............°.   `2`

32–33

d is............., and is approximately............°.   `2`

34   7.49
        + 8.56
        _____   `1`

35   1.78
        + 2.56
        _____   `1`

36   1.68
        + 2.37
        _____   `1`

At a youth club, there are 3 boys for every 4 girls.

37 If there are 12 boys at the club, how many girls are there? ....   `1`

At another youth club, there are also 3 boys for every 4 girls.

38 If there are 12 girls at the club, how many boys are there? ....   `1`

39 How many children altogether go to both youth clubs? ....   `1`

40 How much do I have left from £3.00 after buying 4 flowers at 65p each? . . . . p

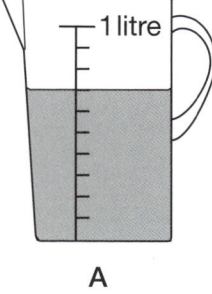 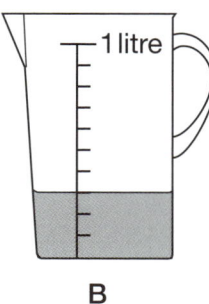 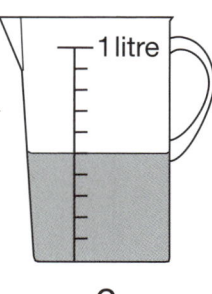

A   B   C

41 B contains . . . . ml.

42 C contains . . . . ml.

43–45

How much is required to fill each jug up to 1 litre?

A . . . . ml   B . . . . ml   C . . . . ml   3

A train departs at 07:49 and arrives at 10:13.

46 How long does the journey take?   . . . . h . . . . min

Here is a plan of our bathroom.

Scale: 2 cm = 1 m

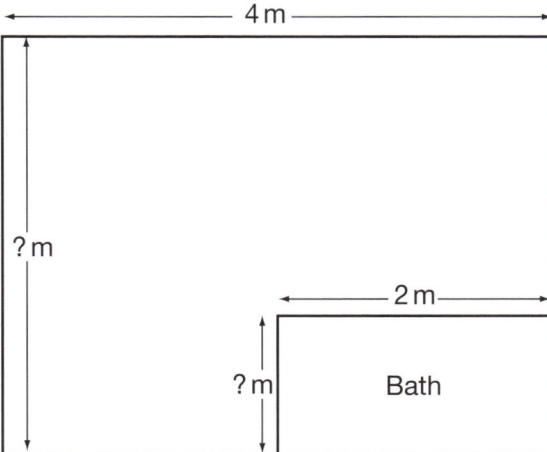

47 What is the perimeter of the bathroom? . . . .

48 We would need . . . . floor tiles of 50 cm × 50 cm to cover the whole floor.   1

50 What is the area of the bath? 1

51 What is the area of the bathroom? 1

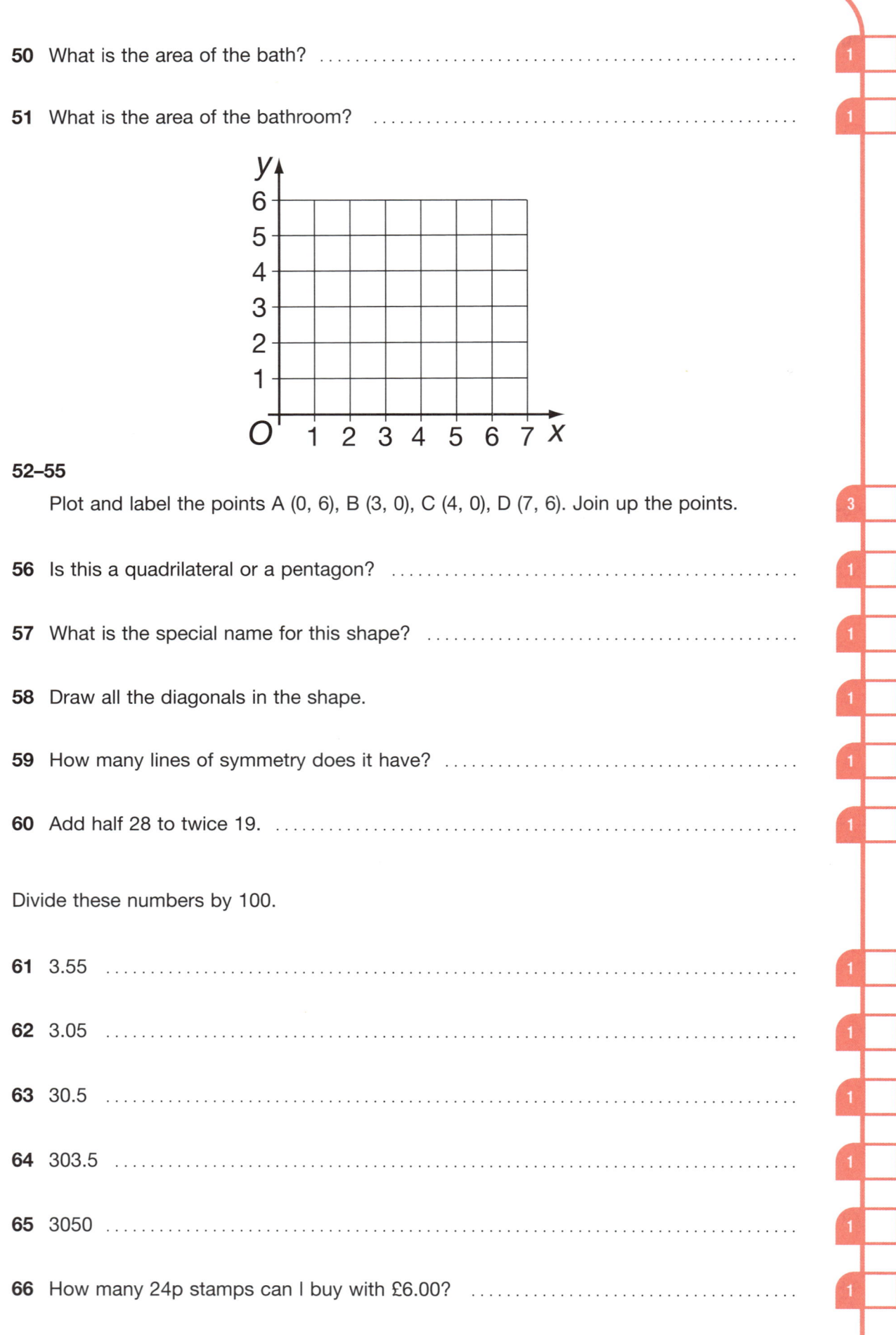

52–55

Plot and label the points A (0, 6), B (3, 0), C (4, 0), D (7, 6). Join up the points. 3

56 Is this a quadrilateral or a pentagon? 1

57 What is the special name for this shape? 1

58 Draw all the diagonals in the shape. 1

59 How many lines of symmetry does it have? 1

60 Add half 28 to twice 19. 1

Divide these numbers by 100.

61 3.55 1

62 3.05 1

63 30.5 1

64 303.5 1

65 3050 1

66 How many 24p stamps can I buy with £6.00? 1

In a class of 30 children, one-tenth do not have school dinners.

67 How many do have them? 1

Find the area of each shape.

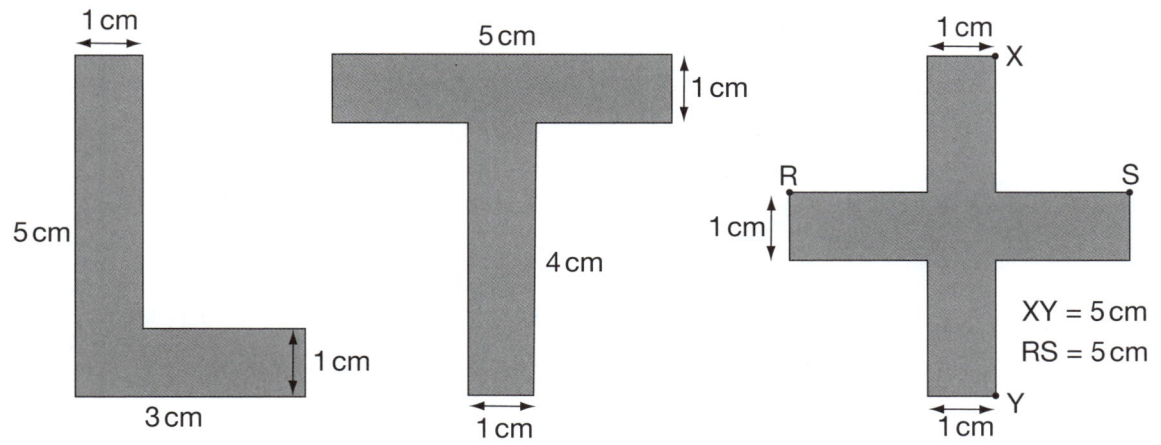

68 ....   **69** **70**   3

71   6.54
   ×   9
   ‾‾‾‾‾‾‾

72   9.500
   + 6.750
   ‾‾‾‾‾‾‾

2

Look at each set of letters below. They form a pattern.

73   a b b r a b b r ...   What would the eleventh letter be? 1

74   b y t o b y b y t ...   What would the tenth letter be?   1

75   x x y z z x x y ...   What would the sixteenth letter be? 1

76–80

Round these numbers to the nearest 100.

    23 432   47 874   35 153   77 077   19 191

    5

Total
80

Keywords

Some special maths words are used in this book. You will find them **in bold** the first time they appear in the book. These words are explained here.

acute angle an angle that is less than a right angle

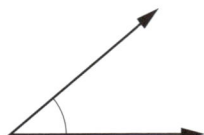

composite a number that has more than 2 factors, so it can be divided by 1, the number itself and at least 1 other number

cube number a number that is made by multiplying the number by itself 3 times

edge the line where two faces join

face a flat side of a solid object

factor the factors of a number are numbers that divide into it with no remainder. For example 1, 2, 4 and 8 are all factors of 8

improper fraction a fraction with the numerator bigger than the denominator

lowest term the simplest you can make a fraction, for example $\frac{4}{10}$ reduced to the lowest term is $\frac{2}{5}$.

mixed number a number that contains a whole number and a fraction, for example $5\frac{1}{2}$ is a mixed number

multiples just extended times tables. They are the original number multiplied by another number

negative number a number that is less than zero and is shown with a minus symbol in front of the number

obtuse angle an angle that is more than 90° and not more than 180°

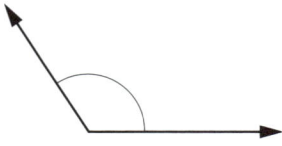

parallel always the same distance apart

polygon   a closed shape with three or more sides

power   the number of times a number is multiplied by itself, for example
                     $3^4 = 3 \times 3 \times 3 \times 3$

prime number   a whole number greater than 1 that has only 2 factors: 1 and the
                     number itself

product   a number or a quantity that you get by multiplying two or more
                     numbers or expressions together

reflex angle   an angle that is bigger than 180° and less than 360°

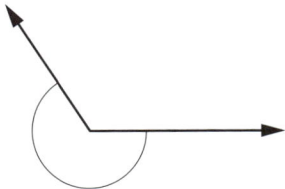

right angle   an angle that is 90°

square number   a number that is made by multiplying the number by itself

vertex, vertices the point where two or more edges or sides in a shape meet

11+ Study Guide

Essentials

- Don't worry too much about the level that you start at. Beginning with an easier book can help your confidence.

- Make sure you have the right equipment – you will need your pencils, an eraser, and a notebook.

- This book contains skills guidance and worked examples, but if you need more help with technique, the Bond Handbooks might also be useful to you.

Studying Effectively

1 Turn to the first topic and read the key skills box. You might want to read it a few times or with someone else to understand it properly or to underline key words.

2 Read the worked example a few times and make sure you understand it.

3 In your notebook, write down the topic heading and the worked example on a new page. This is for you to revise and remember. Once you have completed the final book, you will have a super-useful notebook that you can use in secondary school.

4 Now set a timer – a kitchen timer, a watch or phone with an alarm – for the timed section.

5 Work your way through the questions carefully. If you don't know the answer to something, draw a circle around the question number and take your best guess. This is important as you can find patterns if you make mistakes and it highlights where you need to consolidate.

6 Ask someone to mark the paper for you or mark it yourself and see where you made mistakes. Is there a common pattern? For every mistake, decide if it is not knowing the technique properly, not consolidating the technique enough or a loss of focus and label this next to each question using T = technique, C = consolidation, F = focus.

7 Have another go at the questions you made errors in to understand what you did wrong.

Making Mistakes

Everyone makes mistakes and they are an important part of how we learn. The reason we practise before an exam is so that we can make those mistakes in a safe space rather than in the test itself and, that way, we can learn from them and make fewer mistakes when it really matters.

Remember that there is no such thing as a 'silly mistake'. You are not silly, and neither is your mistake. It is usually not understanding the technique, not consolidating the skill needed so that it is only partially remembered, or you have lost focus. Losing focus does not mean that you have done something bad; it just means that your attention was on something else. These tips can help:

Not Understanding the Technique:

• Go back to the learning section and reread the key skills box.

• Look at the worked example that you have in your notebook.

• Use the Bond Handbook for more support.

Not Consolidating Enough:

• It is amazing how much consolidation is needed by everyone, so don't worry about doing lots of additional questions.

• Look at Bond online for some more questions to help you revise.

• Ask someone to test you on the technique.

Losing Focus:

• Make sure that you are not too tired, hungry, thirsty or distracted.

• Work out where you have made a mistake and break it down into sections. It might be that you focus on tricky division, but go too fast when it comes to addition.

• Once you have identified the problem area, make sure that in new questions, you check yourself and focus carefully.

Common Problems

'I don't have time to study.'
Make sure that you have a timetable that is doable. If you have lots of activities that take up time, perhaps break your work up. The books all have timing sections so fit in smaller sections when you can. It's important to talk to your parent if you feel that you need more time for your 11+ work.

'I find it hard to complete my homework as I want to play instead.'
Motivation is difficult for most people. Don't completely stop all fun activities during the 11+ but get a balance. Key to this is a timetable so you know when, what and where to study. Make sure it is doable and build in something fun if you complete your homework for the day. Another tip is to write down your reasons for doing the 11+. It might be to keep your family happy, to get into a school your friends are going to, or even that the school is convenient. Ask yourself how important each reason is. Can you commit to the reasons you have? If so, keep remembering the reason and what will happen if you don't commit? Perhaps talk to your family so that they know how you feel.

'My friend is using different books to me.'
The Bond 11+ system covers English/Verbal Reasoning and Maths/Non-verbal reasoning/spatial awareness. Bond has had many decades of success in 11+ material. Many tutors will only use Bond for their pupils, and they get an exceptionally high pass rate. It doesn't mean that Bond is the only 11+ provider, so don't worry that your friend is using different material. What is important is that you are fully prepared for your CEM online exam, and you can have confidence in the Bond system.

'I'm scared of failing.'
It is natural to feel that. Remember that you cannot climb a mountain in one gigantic step. You need lots and lots of little steps to get to the top. The 11+ is like that. You can't sit down and learn everything straight away, but the little steps you take will lead you to the exam. Remember that every mistake can be identified and once you identify it, you may be able to understand it and solve the problem for next time. Mistakes are perfection in progress! If a selective school is the best learning environment for you, then you can work little and often through the books and then test papers leading up to the exam. If you find it too much and you are working at your full potential already, then maybe a school that is not selective will suit your learning better. There is no 'best school' and 'worst school' for everyone. It is the best school for an individual child. Do talk to someone about your feelings, though, as you need to feel supported.

'My friend has a tutor. Do I need one?'
Whether or not to have tutor depends on many different factors, including where your particular strengths and challenges lie, your own approach to learning and whether your parents are comfortable with the costs involved. The Bond system is rigorous and aims to support every child with a range of books and learning materials. The Bond Handbooks can do the job of a tutor and many tutors also use the Bond books and Handbooks with their pupils. Bond has been providing 11+ material since the 1960s, helping thousands of pupils to pass their 11+ exams without having a tutor.

'I don't want to do the 11+ exam.'
This is a conversation to have with your family, but the best advice might be to follow the 11+ books anyway. They will teach you skills, techniques and methods that will give you self-confidence regardless of the secondary school you attend. No knowledge is a waste, and you will be keeping your options open. There is more information on the Bond website. Bond has a *Parent's Guide to the 11+* and there is a range of supportive printed and online material. See online for further details. **www.bond11plus.co.uk**

Answers

Learning Paper: Basic Number Skills

Types of numbers

	11	12
multiples	11, 22, 33, …	12, 24, 36, …
factors	1, 11	1, 2, 3, 4, 6, 12
prime factors	11	$2 \times 2 \times 3$
composite		1, 2, 3, 4, 6, 12
prime	1×11	

1 **910** $35 \times 26 = 910$

```
          3 5
  ×       2 6
        2 1 0
          3
  +     7 0 0
        1
        9 1 0
```

2 **864 332** The largest digit should go in the most significant place value column, so in this case the 8 will go in the hundred thousands column. The next largest digit should go in the next place value column, so 6 will go in the ten thousands column. Continue putting the next largest digit in the next place value column.

3 **10 014** There is 1 ten thousand, 1 ten and 4 ones. Remember to put zeros in the thousands and hundreds places.

4 **101 000** There is 1 hundred thousand and 1 thousand. Remember to put zeros in the ten thousands, hundreds, tens and ones places.

5 **9000** The 5 in 8536 means that when rounded up the number is 9000.

6 **8500** The 3 in 8536 means that when rounded down the number is 8500.

7 **8000** The 6 in 7680 means that when rounded up the number is 8000.

8 **4540** The 5 in 4535 means that when rounded up to the nearest 10 the number is 4540.

9 **7** $2 \times 7 = 14$

10–12 **18, 2, 9** $1 \times 18 = 18$; $2 \times 9 = 18$

13–16 **32, 40, 48, 56** $8 \times 4 = 32$; $8 \times 5 = 40$; $8 \times 6 = 48$; $8 \times 7 = 56$

17 **17** $2 + 3 + 5 + 7 = 17$

18 **6** $29 - 23 = 6$

19 **6** $37 - 31 = 6$

20 **–2.5** The arrow is pointing halfway between –2 and –3.

21–22 **–6, –3** $-4 - 2 = -6$, $-6 + 3 = -3$

23 **64** $8 \times 8 = 64$

24 **121** $11^2 = 11 \times 11 = 121$

25 **9** $9 \times 9 = 81$

Learning Paper: Using the Four Operations

1 **274** 98 has been increased by 100 and 76 has not been changed, so the answer will increase by 100 ($174 + 100 = 274$).

2 **474** 98 has been increased by 300 and 76 has not been changed, so the answer will increase by 300 ($174 + 300 = 474$).

3 **674** 98 has been increased by 400 and 76 has been increased 100, so the answer will increase by 500 ($174 + 500 = 674$).

4 **17.72** $4.68 + 9.25 + 3.79 = 17.72$

```
          4 · 6 8
          9 · 2 5
  +       3 · 7 9
      1 7 · 7 2
      1   1   2
```

5 **26.07** $14.37 + 11.70 = 26.07$

```
    1 4 · 3 7
  + 1 1 · 7 0
    2 6 · 0 7
        1
```

6 **0.1** 0.9 is the same as 0.90 so:

```
    ⁰1 · ¹0 0
  -  0 · 9 0
     0 · 1 0
```

7 **1961** $2010 - 49 = 1961$

```
    ¹2 ⁹0 ¹0+ 0
  -         4 9
    1 9 6 1
```

8 **1.36** $4.12 - 2.76 = 1.36$

```
    ¹4 · ¹0+ ¹2
  -  2 ·  7 6
     1 ·  3 6
```

9 **7061** $7500 - 439 = 7061$

```
    7 ⁴5 ⁹0 ¹0
  -     4 3 9
    7 0 6 1
```

10 **5994** $7001 - 1007 = 5994$

```
    ⁵7 ⁹0 ⁹0 ¹1
  -  1 0 0 7
     5 9 9 4
```

11 **24** 4 sixes means 4×6.

12 **27** 3 lots of 9 means 3×9.

13 **56** 7 times 8 means 7×8.

14 **44 660** $145 \times 308 = 44\ 660$

```
        1  4  5
    ×   3  0  8
    1  1  6  0
       3  4
       0  0  0
 4  3  5  0  0
    1  1
 4  4  6  6  0
```

15 **49.36** $6.17 \times 8 = 49.36$

```
      6  ·  1  7
   ×     ·     8
   4  9  ·  3  6
         1     5
```

16 $6\overline{)50}$ = 8 rem 2 $6 \times 8 = 48; 48 + 2 = 50$

17–18 $7\overline{)68}$ = 9 rem 5 $7 \times 9 = 63; 63 + 5 = 68$

19 **3.49** $27.92 \div 8 = 3.49$

```
      0  3  ·  4  9
 8 | 2  ²7  ·  ³9  ⁷2
```

20–21 **21 ÷ 6, 19 ÷ 4** $6 \times 3 = 18$ and $18 + 3 = 21$; $4 \times 4 = 16$ and $16 + 3 = 19$

22 **16** Half of 8 = 4; twice 6 = 12; 12 + 4 = 16

23 **2452** *See answers to questions 1–3.*

24 **3563** *See answer to question 10.*

25 **6** A product is found by multiplying numbers together; $7 \times 6 = 42$

Learning Paper: Fractions, Decimals and Percentages

1 **20** $2 \times 2 = 4; 10 \times 2 = 20$

2 **7** $\frac{5}{5} = 1; \frac{7}{7} = 1$

3 **8** $\frac{3}{5} = \frac{1}{2} = \frac{4}{8}$

4–6 To add or subtract fractions with the same denominators, only add and subtract the numerators, not the denominators.

4 **$\frac{4}{5}$** $\frac{2}{10} + \frac{7}{10} - \frac{1}{10} = \frac{8}{10} = \frac{4}{5}$

5 **$\frac{1}{2}$** $\frac{9}{10} - \frac{6}{10} + \frac{2}{10} = \frac{5}{10} = \frac{1}{2}$

6 **$\frac{99}{100}$** $\frac{9}{100} + \frac{90}{100} = \frac{99}{100}$

7 **$\frac{1}{2}$** The shape is split into 2 equal pieces, 1 of which is shaded.

8 **$\frac{3}{5}$** The shape is split into 5 equal pieces, 3 of which are shaded.

9 **$\frac{1}{2}$** The shape is split into 16 equal pieces, 8 of which are shaded. $\frac{8}{16} = \frac{1}{2}$

10 **5** 1 whole = 2 halves; $2 + \frac{1}{2} = 2 \times 2$ halves + 1 half = 5 halves

11 **7** 1 whole = 4 quarters; $1 + \frac{3}{4} = 4$ quarters + 3 quarters = 7 quarters

12 **360** If $\frac{3}{5}$ are boys, then $\frac{2}{5}$ are girls. Divide the number of girls by 2 to find $\frac{1}{5}$ ($240 \div 2 = 120$, so $\frac{1}{5} = 120$). Multiply 120 by 3 to find $\frac{3}{5}$ ($120 \times 3 = 360$).

13 **600** $240 + 360 = 600$

14 **60** To find one-twelfth of an amount divide the amount by 12 ($720 \div 12 = 60$).

15–16 The symbol < means 'is less than'. The symbol > means 'is greater than'.

15 **<**

16 **>**

17–18 To multiply by 100, place the numbers in a decimal grid using hundreds, tens, ones, tenths, hundredths, thousandths, etc. Multiply a number by 100 by moving it two places to the left.

17 **24**

H	T	O	·	t	h
		0	·	2	4
	2	4			

18 **0.76**

H	T	O	·	t	h	th	hth
		0	·	0	0	7	6
		0	·	7	6		

19 **5** There are 100 pence in a pound; $20 \times 5 = 100$

20 **4** If there are 100 pence in £1.00, there are 200 pence in £2.00. $50 \times 4 = 200$

21 **50** If there are 100 pence in £1.00, there are 500 pence in £5.00. $10 \times 50 = 500$

22 **44** 50% + 25% = 75% and 100% − 75% = 25%, so 25% of the counters are white; 25% = 11 counters. $25\% \times 4 = 100\%$, so multiply 11 by 4 to find out how many counters there are altogether; $11 \times 4 = 44$

23 **330** 100% − 40% = 60% are children. First find 10% by dividing by 10 ($550 \div 10 = 55$). Then multiply by 6 to find 60% ($55 \times 6 = 330$).

24–25 Place the numbers in a decimal grid using hundreds, tens, ones, tenths, hundredths, thousandths, etc. To divide a number by 10 move it one place to the right on the grid; to divide by 100 move it two places to the right.

24 **0.1** $\frac{1}{10} = 1 \div 10 = 0.1$

H	T	O	·	t	h
		1	·		
		0	·	1	

25 **0.03** $\frac{3}{100} = 3 \div 100 = 0.03$

H	T	O	·	t	h
		3			
		0	·	0	3

Learning Paper: Sequences and Basic Algebra Skills

1–12 First work out the sequence between the numbers. Then use the same rule to find the next two numbers.

1–2 **90, 120** The sequence is to add 5, then add 10, then add 15 and so on; 65 + 25 = 90; 90 + 30 = 120

3–4 **11, 12$\frac{1}{2}$** The sequence is to add 1$\frac{1}{2}$. So 9$\frac{1}{2}$ + 1$\frac{1}{2}$ = 11; 11 + 1$\frac{1}{2}$ = 12$\frac{1}{2}$

5–6 **2.1 or 2.10, 2.15** The sequence is to add 0.05; 2.05 + 0.05 = 2.1; 2.1 + 0.05 = 2.15

7–8 **22, 29** The sequence is to add 2, then add 3, then add 4, and so on; 16 + 6 = 22; 22 + 7 = 29

9–10 **12, 5** The sequence is to subtract 12, then subtract 11, then subtract 10, and so on; 20 – 8 = 12; 12 – 7 = 5

11–12 **12.34, 1.234** The sequence is to divide by 10; 123.4 ÷ 10 = 12.34; 12.34 ÷ 10 = 1.234.

13–14 **÷, +** 57 ÷ 3 = 19, 19 = 2 + 17

15–16 **–, ×** 57 – 13 = 44, 44 = 11 × 4

17–18 **+, ÷** 57 + 3 = 60, 60 = 120 ÷ 2

19 **5** In this type of question, work backwards through the sum. What number must be divided by 3 to make 2? (6 ÷ 3 = 2) Then work out which number is added to 1 to make 6; 5 + 1 = 6

20 **16** 6 – 2 = 4; 4 × 4 = 16

21 **11** 50 – 6 = 44; 44 ÷ 4 = 11

22 **26** 43 – 17 = 26

23–24 **4, 42** 23 – ? = 19 or ? – 23=19; so 23 – 19 = ? or ? = 23 + 19

25 **19** 70 – 3x = 13; so 3x = 70 – 13 = 57, and 57 ÷ 3 = 19

Learning Paper: Measures

1 **15 m²** The area of a rectangle can be found by multiplying the length by the width (5 × 3 = 15).

2 **4** There are 100 centimetres in 1 metre, so the area of the square is 100 cm × 100 cm = 10 000 cm². The area of one tile is 50 cm × 50 cm = 2500 cm². Divide the area of the square by the area of one tile to find how many will fit (10 000 ÷ 2500 = 4).

3 **60** There are 10 000 cm² in 1 m², so 15 m² = 150 000 cm²; 150 000 ÷ 2500 = 60

4–6 The perimeter of a rectangle can be found by adding up the 2 lengths and the 2 widths.

	Length	Width	Perimeter
Rectangle 1	7 m	5 m	**24 m**
Rectangle 2	6 m	**4 m**	20 m
Rectangle 3	**8 m**	3 m	22 m

7 **8.75 m²** When multiplying decimals, remove the decimal point and multiply the numbers. (2.5 ×3.5 becomes 25 × 35 = 875). Then count the amount of numbers after the decimal point in the question: there are 2 numbers after the decimal points in the question, so there must be 2 numbers after the decimal point in the answer (2.5 × 3.5 = 8.75).

8 **3.5 m** 14 ÷ 4 = 3.5

9 **70 (volume)** 7 × 5 × 2 = 70

10 **4 (width)** 8 × ? × 3 = 96; so 24 × ? = 96 and ? = 96 ÷ 24 = 4

11 **6 (height)** Make sure you convert the 1.2 cm to 12 mm first. 2 × 12 × ? = 120, so 24 × ? = 120 and ? = 120 ÷ 24 = 6

12–13 **4.5 or 4$\frac{1}{2}$, 3.5 or 3$\frac{1}{2}$** On the diagram the bedroom is 4.5 m long and 3.5 m wide.

14 **1.5 or 1$\frac{1}{2}$** On the plan, 1 cm represents 1 m, so 2 cm represents 2 m, 3 cm represents 3 m and so on. Using a ruler, the length of the window is 1.5 cm and the length of the bed is 2 cm.

15 **8** There are 1000 grams in a kilogram, so to convert kilograms to grams, multiply by 1000 (2 kg = 2000 g; 2000 g ÷ 250 g = 8).

16 **23.776** Change all the given measures into grams. There are 1000 g in 1 kg so: 9 kg = 9000 g; 14.5 kg = 14 500g; 276 g stays the same. 9000 g + 276 g + 14 500 g = 23 776 g. Then turn the grams in kg: 23 776 g ÷ 1000 = 23.776 kg

17 **1238.408** Change all the given measures into kg then add them together. 408 g = 0.408 kg; 1.23 tonnes = 1230 kg. 8 + 0.408 + 1230 = 1238.408 kg

18–19 There are 10 increments between 0 and 1 litre. There are 1000 millilitres in 1 litre. Divide 1000 ml by the number of increments (1000 ÷ 10 = 100 ml). So each increment represents 100 ml.

18 **900 ml**

19 **700 ml**

20 **100 ml** Subtract the amount in the jug from 1000 ml. 1000 – 900 = 100

21 **91** In a leap year February has 29 days. January has 31 days and March has 31 days; 31 + 31 + 29 = 91

22 **4** 9 o'clock until noon is 3 hours. 2 p.m. until 3:30 p.m. is 1.5 hours. 3 hours + 1.5 hours = 4.5 hours. There are two 15-minute breaks: 2 × 15 minutes = 30 minutes = 0.5 hours. 4.5 hours – 0.5 hours = 4 hours

23 **12:11 p.m.** 11:57 a.m. + 3 minutes = 12:00 p.m.; 12:00 p.m. + 11 minutes = 12:11 p.m.

24–25 The symbol > means greater than. The symbol < means less than.

24 **>** 4.09 km × 1000 = 4090 m; 4100 m > 4090 m.

25 **<** 1.009 litres × 1000 = 1009 ml; 999 ml < 1009 ml.

Learning Paper: Shape, Space, Position and Direction

1–4 Parallel lines are always the same distance from each other and will never meet or touch.

1 **2**

2 **1**

3 **4**

4 **0**

5–7 A face is a flat surface of a 3D shape, an edge is the straight line where 2 faces meet and a vertex is a corner where 2 or more faces meet.

	A	B
Number of faces	6	**7**
Number of vertices	**8**	10
Number of edges	12	**15**

8 **55°** Angles on a straight line add up to 180° (180° − 90° − 35° = 55°).

9 **30°** Angles on a straight line add up to 180° (180° − 90°, so 3*b* = 90°; 90° ÷ 3 = 30°).

10 **90°** A full turn = 360°. From N to E is a quarter turn (360° ÷ 4 = 90°).

11 **180°** A full turn = 360°. From N to S is a half turn (360° ÷ 2 = 180°).

12 **135°** A full turn = 360°. From SE to S is of a turn (360° ÷ 8 = 45°). From SE to W is 3 lots of 45° (3 × 45° = 135°).

13–16 An acute angle is less than 90°. A right angle is exactly 90°. An obtuse angle is greater than 90° but less than 180°.

13 **Acute**

14 **Obtuse**

15 **Right angle**

16 **Obtuse**

17–20 **A, C, F, G** If a shape has a line of symmetry, the sides on either side of the line will be the same length.

21–24 When plotting coordinates on a grid, use the rule 'along the corridor and up the stairs' to remember to go horizontal, then vertical.

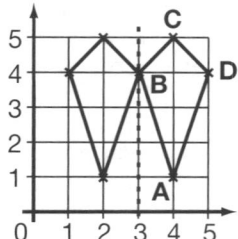

25 **1** If a shape has a line of symmetry, the sides on either side of the line will be identical.

Learning Paper: Statistics

1 **25** Add up all the numbers in the Venn diagram (6 + 5 + 4 + 4 + 1 + 2 + 3 = 25).

2 **4** Add the numbers in the overlap between the oval for blue T-shirts and the oval for white trainers (3 + 1 = 4).

3 **3** Find the number in the overlap of all 3 ovals.

4 **2** Find the overlap between the oval for white trainers and the oval for striped socks. Ignore the number that is also in the overlapped oval for blue T-shirts (3).

5 **18** Add up all the numbers in the Venn diagram (6 + 3 + 5 + 4 = 18).

6 **9** Add up all the numbers in the oval for dark hair (3 + 6 = 9).

7 **8** Add up all the numbers in the oval for brown eyes (3 + 5 = 8).

8 **3** Find the overlap between the oval for brown eyes and the oval for dark hair.

9 **9** There are 18 children, 9 of whom do have dark hair; 18 − 9 = 9.

10–11 **Wednesday, Sunday** On both Wednesday and Sunday the bar representing BBC1 (light grey) and the bar representing ITV1 (dark grey) are the same height.

12 **Friday** On Friday the difference between the bar representing BBC1 (light grey) and the bar representing ITV1 (dark grey) is greater than on any other day.

13 **Monday** BBC1 is represented by the light grey bar. This bar is lowest on Monday.

14 **Tuesday** ITV1 is represented by the dark grey bar. This bar is lowest on Tuesday.

15 **Wednesday** Wednesday is the lowest point on the line graph.

16–17 **Thursday, Saturday** The snow level increased from 4 cm on Wednesday to 6 cm on Thursday. The snow level increased from 6 cm on Friday to 8 cm on Saturday.

18–19 **Monday, Tuesday** The snow level on Monday and Tuesday was 12 cm which is greater than 10 cm. On all other days the snow level was lower than 10 cm.

20 **No** There are no days when the level of snow is more than 20 cm.

21–25 The key states that the drawing represents 1 child.

21 **9**

22 **5**

23 **2**

24 **3** 7 − 4 = 3

25 $\frac{1}{3}$ **or** $\frac{9}{27}$ There are 27 children in total, 9 of whom live on High street $\left(\frac{9}{27} = \frac{1}{3}\right)$.

Learning Paper: Words and Logic Problems

1 **£1.20** 3 × 40p = 120p = £1.20

2 **£4.80** If 1 book is 4 weeks late the fine is 4 × 40 = 160p. If 3 books are 4 weeks late the fine is so 3 × 160 = 480p = £4.80

3 **£6.80** If 1 book is 5 weeks late the fine is 5 × 40 = 200p. If 1 book is 6 weeks late the fine is 6 × 40p = 240p, so if 2 books are 6 weeks late the fine is 2 × 240p = 480p. In total, 200p + 480p = 680p = £6.80

4 **165** If $1.65 is equivalent to £1, multiply both numbers by 100 to find out how many dollars there are for £100 ($1.65 × 100 = $165).

5 **9500** If 190 rupees is equivalent to £1, multiply both numbers by 50 to find out how many rupees there are for £50 (190 rupees × 50 = 9500 rupees).

6 **36** If €1.2 is equivalent to £1, multiply both numbers by 30 to find out how many euros there are for £30 (€1.2 × 30 = €36).

7 **2** £1 = 190; 380 ÷ 190 = 2

8 **306** If $1.53 is equal to £1, multiply both numbers by 200 to find out how many dollars there are for £200 ($1.53 × 200 = $306).

9 **605** If 121 Shillings is equal to £1, multiply both numbers by 5 to find out how many shillings there are for £5 (121 × 5 = 605 shillings).

10 **100** If A\$1.72 is equal to £1, divide A\$172 by 1.72 to find how many pounds you get (172 ÷ 1.72 = £100).

11 **90 m** 1 minute = 60 seconds; 2 minutes = 2 × 60 = 120 seconds; 120 ÷ 20 = 6; 15m × 6 = 90 m

12 **08:35 or 8:35 a.m.** $\frac{1}{4}$ of an hour = 15 minutes; 8:50 a.m. – 15 minutes = 8:35 a.m.

13 **42** Remember to multiply both the decimal numbers you are dividing into by the same power of 10. 50.4 ÷ 1.2 is the same as 504 ÷ 12 = 42

14 **28p, 33p, 37p** 28p = 20p + 5p + 2p + 1p; 33p = 20p + 10p + 2p + 1p; 37p = 20p + 10p + 5p + 2p

15–17 To find the number halfway between two numbers, add the two numbers together and then divide by 2.

15 **25** 20 + 30 = 50; 50 ÷ 2 = 25

16 **28** 21 + 35 = 56; 56 ÷ 2 = 28

17 **23** 17 + 29 = 46; 46 ÷ 2 = 23

18 **10** 14 × 27 = 378; 378 – 368 = 10

19 **32** The area of a rectangle can be found by multiplying the length by the width, so the area of the card is 20 cm × 40 cm = 800 cm² and the area of one square is 5 cm × 5 cm = 25 cm². Divide the area of the card by the area of one square to find how many will fit (800 ÷ 25 = 32).

20–21 The ratio of present to absent is 6 : 1. To solve a ratio, add up the ratio numbers (6 + 1 = 7). Then divide this number into the number of children (28 ÷ 7 = 4). Finally, multiply this number by the individual ratios.

20 **24** 6 × 4 = 24

21 **4** 1 × 4 = 4

22 **8p** 91p – 75p = 16p; 16p ÷ 2 = 8p

23 **83p** 91p – 8p = 83p and 75p + 8p = 83p

24–25 You need 2 numbers with a difference of 8, such as 1 and 9. The sum of 1 and 9 is 10, but we need it to be 26. We want another 16, so each number has to be 8 bigger, so 9 and 17.

24 **17** 26 ÷ 2 = 13; 8 ÷ 2 = 4; 13 + 4 = 17

25 **9** 26 ÷ 2 = 13; 8 ÷ 2 = 4; 13 – 4 = 9

Curveball Questions 1

1 **3 and 6** The pattern is going downwards from the top row to the bottom row. 3 is added to each digit in the top row and the answer is shown in the digit in the row directly below:

1	5	3	2	4	6
+3	+3	+3	+3	+3	+3
4	8	6	5	7	9

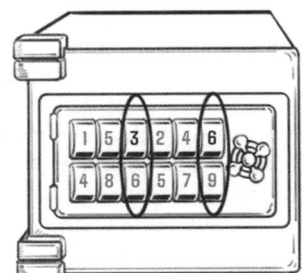

2 **6** There are 3 dogs with pointy ears and 2 with floppy black ears.
Ignore the dogs that don't fit the description, then give each of the other dogs a letter.

A   B   C   D   E

If you had to choose 1 dog with pointy ears and 1 with floppy black ears, you could have dogs A and B, or A and C, or A and D, or B and E, or C and E, or D and E. So there are 6 options.

Mixed Paper 1

1–5

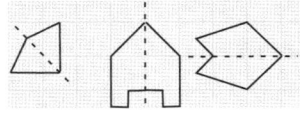 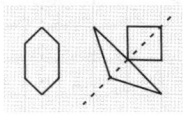

6 **8** 8 × 8 = 64

7 **$\frac{3}{4}$** To add fractions, first find equivalent fractions so that the bottom numbers (the denominators) are the same in both fractions: $\frac{1}{2} = \frac{2}{4}$. Remember to only add the top numbers (the numerators), not the denominators. $\frac{2}{4} + \frac{1}{4} = \frac{3}{4}$.

8 **45** 6 × 7 = 42; 42 + 3 = 45

9 **3.5 m or $3\frac{1}{2}$ m** 28 ÷ 8 = 3 r 4 = $3\frac{4}{8} = 3\frac{1}{2}$ or 3.5

10 **864 320** The largest digit should go in the most significant place value column, so in this case the 8 will go in the hundred thousands column. The next largest digit should go in the next place value column, so 6 will go in the ten thousands column. Continue putting the next largest digit in the next place value column.

11 **eight hundred and sixty-four thousand three hundred and twenty** Read the number from left to right, starting with the hundred thousands place value column.

12 **15** 1 whole = 2 halves; $7 + \frac{1}{2} = 7 × 2$ halves + 1 half = 14 halves + 1 half = 15 halves

13 **21** 1 whole = 2 halves; $10 + \frac{1}{2} = 10 × 2$ halves + 1 half = 20 halves + 1 half = 21 halves

14 **46** 1 whole = 2 halves; 23 × 2 halves = 46 halves

15 **10** There are 1000 millilitres in 1 litre and 1000 ÷ 4 = 250, so $\frac{1}{4}$ litre = 250 ml; 2.5 × 1000 = 2500, so 2.5 litres = 2500 ml; 2500 ÷ 250 = 10

16 **11 h 45 min** From 7:30 p.m. to 7:15 a.m. the next day is 15 minutes less than 12 hours.

17 **9 km²** 3 km × 3 km = 9 km²

18 **12 km** 3 km + 3 km + 3 km + 3 km = 12 km

19 **4 km** A square has four sides of equal length. 16 ÷ 4 = 4 km

20 **16 km** 4 km + 4 km + 4 km + 4 km = 16 km

21 **12** There are 60 minutes in 1 hour; 60 ÷ 5 = 12

22 **5** There are 100 cm in 1 metre; 100 ÷ 20 = 5

23 **8** There are 1000 ml in 1 litre; 1000 ÷ 125 = 8

24 20 There are 1000 m in 1 km; 1000 ÷ 50 = 20

25 93.04 78.05 + 9.92 + 5.07 = 93.04

```
      7 8 · 0 5
        9 · 9 2
  +     5 · 0 7
  ───────────────
      9 3 · 0 4
      2 1     1
```

26 45 9.5 cm + 13 cm + 9.5 cm + 13 cm = 45 cm

27 74 37 × 2 = 74

28 1.560 or 1.56 9.420 − 7.860 = 1.56

```
    ⁸9 · ¹³4 ¹2 0
  −  7 · 8 6 0
  ───────────────
     1 · 5 6 0
```

29 35p Divide 21p by 3 to find $\frac{1}{5}$ (21p ÷ 3 = 7p). Multiply this by 5 to find the full amount (7p × 5 = 35p).

30 54 36 ÷ 2 = 18; 18 × 3 = 54

31 30 $\frac{1}{5}$ = 6; multiply 6 by 5 to find the total (6 × 5 = 30).

32 6 h 30 min 50 km/h means 50 km in 1 hour. To get to 300 km we need at least 50 + 50 + 50 + 50 + 50 + 50 km. 50 km/h × 6 = 300 km. Half of 50 km/h = 25 km/h, so 25 km/h = 30 minutes. Add 6 hours and 30 minutes together to get the answer.

33 12.78 Change 13 m into cm by multiplying by 100: 13 × 100 = 1300 cm. 1300 cm − 22 cm = 1278 cm. Then change the measurement back into metres by dividing by 100: 1278 cm ÷ 100 = 12.78 m

34 24 10 + 2 + 3 + 1 + 7 + 1 = 24

35 $\frac{1}{8}$ 3 children out of 24 prefer rabbits. $\frac{3}{24} = \frac{1}{8}$

36 10

37 1

38 3 10 − 7 = 3

39 0.22 22 ÷ 100 = 0.22

40 0.44 $\frac{22}{50} = \frac{44}{100}$; 44 ÷ 100 = 0.44

Mixed Paper 2

1 50% The garden is split into 8 equal pieces, 4 of which are lawn. $\frac{4}{8} = \frac{1}{2}$ = 50%

2 $\frac{1}{8}$ The garden is split into 8 equal pieces, 1 of which is cabbages: $\frac{1}{8}$.

3 25% The garden is split into 8 equal pieces, 2 of which are for potatoes. $\frac{2}{8} = \frac{1}{4}$ = 25%

4 $\frac{1}{8}$ The garden is split into 8 equal pieces, 1 of which is carrots.

5–6 The area of a rectangle can be found by multiplying the length by the width.

5 1800 60 × 30 = 1800

6 900 The lawn is half the length of the garden. Half of 60 is 30, so the lawn is 30 m long and 30 m wide; 30 × 30 = 900

7 9 3^2 = 3 × 3 = 9

8 6 There are 60 minutes in an hour; 10 × 6 = 60

9 $3\frac{1}{2}$ $\frac{1}{2}$ of 7 = $\frac{1}{2} \times 7 = \frac{7}{2} = 3\frac{1}{2}$

10 10.5 or $10\frac{1}{2}$ litres 105 ÷ 10 = 10.5

11 10 To solve a ratio, add up the ratio numbers (3 + 2 = 5). Then divide this number into the number of children (25 ÷ 5 = 5). Finally, multiply this number by 2 to find the number of girls (2 × 5 = 10).

12–14 When plotting coordinates on a grid, use the rule 'along the corridor and up the stairs' to remember to go horizontal, then vertical.

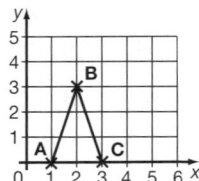

15 Isosceles triangle The shape has 3 sides, 2 of which are equal in length.

16 1 If a shape has a line of symmetry, the sides on either side of the line will be identical.

17 Move each point on the triangle 2 units to the right.

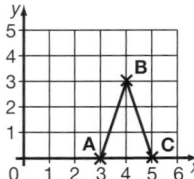

18 c 5 letters are being repeated in a pattern, a b c d e. Therefore, the letter a will be the first, sixth, eleventh and sixteenth letter. b will be the seventeenth and c will be the eighteenth letter.

19 x 3 letters are being repeated in a pattern, x y z. Therefore, x will be the first, fourth, seventh and tenth letter.

20 $\frac{5}{8}$ $\frac{1}{2} = \frac{4}{8}$; $\frac{1}{8} + \frac{4}{8} = \frac{5}{8}$

21 91 7 × 13 = 91

22 51 3 × 17 = 51

23 143 11 × 13 = 143

24 27 6^2 = 6 × 6 = 36; 3^2 = 3 × 3 = 9; 36 − 9 = 27

25 11:57 a.m. The clock loses a minute every day. Noon Monday to noon Thursday is 3 days, so in 3 days the clock will lose 3 × 1 minute = 3 minutes. 3 minutes before noon is 11:57 a.m.

26 12 356 The smallest digit should go in the most significant place value column, so in this case the 1 goes in the ten thousands column. The second-smallest digit should go in the next place value column, so 2 goes in the thousands column. Continue putting the next smallest digit in the next place value column.

27 12 365 The smallest possible number that can be made using these digits (12 356) is even. To make it odd, swap the last even digit (6) with the last odd digit (5).

28 65 321 The largest digit should go in the most significant place value column, so in this case the 6 goes in the ten thousands column. The second-largest digit should go in the next place value column, so 5 goes in the thousands column. Continue putting the next largest digit in the next place value column.

29 **65 312** The largest possible number that can be made using these digits (65 321) is odd. To make it even, swap the last odd digit (1) with the last even digit (2).

30–31 The symbol < means less than. The symbol > means greater than.

30 <

31 >

32 **93** 120 − 27 = 93

$$
\begin{array}{r}
^0{\not{1}}\ ^{11}2\ ^10 \\
-\quad 2\ 7 \\
\hline
0\ 9\ 3
\end{array}
$$

33 **2.9** 3.5 − 0.6 = 2.9

$$
\begin{array}{r}
^23\ \cdot\ ^15 \\
-\ 0\ \cdot\ 6 \\
\hline
2\ \cdot\ 9
\end{array}
$$

34 **173** 5.2 m × 100 = 520 cm; 520 cm − 347 cm = 173 cm

35 **261** 87 + 65 + 46 + 38 + 25 = 261

$$
\begin{array}{r}
8\ 7 \\
6\ 5 \\
4\ 6 \\
3\ 8 \\
+\quad 2\ 5 \\
\hline
2\ 6\ 1 \\
{\scriptstyle 3}
\end{array}
$$

36–38 The key shows that 1 image of a person represents 50 people.

36 **350** 7 × 50 = 350

37 **275** 5 × 50 = 250; half of 50 = 25; 250 + 25 = 275

38 **175** Thursday: 6 × 50 = 300; Wednesday: 2 × 50 = 100 and 100 + 25 = 125. 300 − 125 = 175

39 **10** 6 × 7 = 42; 420 ÷ 42 = 10

40 **50** 2 × 3 = 6; 300 ÷ 6 = 50

Mixed Paper 3

1 $\frac{2}{3}$ The shape is split into 3 equal pieces, 2 of which are shaded.

2 $\frac{1}{2}$ The shape is split into 2 equal pieces, 1 of which is shaded.

3 $\frac{1}{4}$ The shape is split into 4 equal pieces, 1 of which is dotted.

4 $\frac{1}{2}$ Divide the dotted diamond into 4 equal triangles with a cross. The rectangle is now split into 8 equal triangles, 4 of which are dotted. $\frac{4}{8} = \frac{1}{2}$

5 $\frac{18}{35}$ The shape is split into 35 equal pieces, 18 of which are shaded.

6 **180** Divide by 5 to find $\frac{1}{5}$ (300 ÷ 5 = 60) and multiply by 3 to find $\frac{3}{5}$ (60 × 3 = 180).

7 **120** Subtract the number of boys from the total to find the number of girls (300 − 180 = 120).

8 **Paul** 6.70 m is longer than 5.84 m.

9 **86 cm** There are 100 centimetres in 1 metre, so to convert from metres to centimetres, multiply by 100 (6.70 × 100 = 670; 5.84 × 100 = 584; 670 − 584 = 86).

10–13 When rounding a number to the nearest 1000, look at the number in the hundreds column. If it is 4 or below, leave the number in the thousands column unchanged. If it is 5 or above, raise the number in the thousands column by 1. When rounding a number to the nearest 100, look at the number in the tens column. When rounding a number to the nearest 10, look at the number in the ones column.

10 **8000** The 5 in 7583 rounds the number up to 8000.

11–13 **6000, 5900, 5900** The 9 in 5904 rounds the number up to 6000. The 0 in 5904 rounds the number down to 5900. The 4 in 5904 rounds the number down to 5900.

14 **712** 712 − 368 = 344 so, using the inverse operation, 368 + 344 = 712

15 **357** 357 + 345 = 702 so, using the inverse operation, 702 − 345 = 357

16 **344** It is given in the question that 712 − 368 = 344

17 **345** 357 + 345 = 702 so, using the inverse operation, 702 − 357 = 345

18 **368** 712 − 368 = 344 so, using the inverse operation, 712 − 344 = 368

19–22 The first row has a 56, and a 42 and a 77. These are all multiples of 7, so the heading for that row must be 7 and the heading for the first column must be 8 (7 × 8 = 56), the heading for the second column must be 6 (7 × 6 = 42) and the heading for the fourth column must be 11 (7 × 11 = 77). Use logic to fill in the rest of the table.

×	(8)	(6)	(4)	(11)
(7)	56	42	**28**	77
(8)	**64**	48	32	88
(9)	72	**54**	36	**99**

23 **6** A square has 4 equal sides; 24 ÷ 4 = 6

24 **9p or £0.09** The 250 g tin costs 99p. Two 125 g tins cost £1.08 (54p × 2). £1.08 − 99p = £0.09 (or 9p)

25 **31p or £0.31** The 5007 g tin costs £1.85. Four 125 g tins cost £2.16 (54p × 4). £2.16 − £1.85 = £0.31 (or 31p).

26 **9:10 a.m.** A quarter of an hour = 15 minutes; 8:55 a.m. + 15 minutes = 9:10 a.m.

27–28 **0.5 or $\frac{1}{2}$, 0.25 or $\frac{1}{4}$** The sequence is to divide by 2. 1 ÷ 2 = 0.5 or $\frac{1}{2}$. 0.5 ÷ 2 = 0.25 or $\frac{1}{2} \div 2 = \frac{1}{4}$

29–30 **2, 2.25** The sequence is to add 0.25. 1.75 + 0.25 = 2. 2 + 0.25 = 2.25.

31–32 **12, 18** To solve a ratio, add up the ratio numbers (2 + 3 = 5). Then divide this number into the number of children (30 ÷ 5 = 6). Finally, multiply this number by the individual ratios (2 × 6 = 12 girls, 3 × 6 = 18 boys).

33 **7474** 9191 – 1717 = 7474

34 **157** $6^2 = 6 \times 6 = 36$; $11^2 = 11 \times 11 = 121$; 36 + 121 = 157

35 **85** $9^2 = 9 \times 9 = 81$; $2^2 = 2 \times 2 = 4$; 81 + 4 = 85

36 **208** $8^2 = 8 \times 8 = 64$; $12^2 = 12 \times 12 = 144$; 64 + 144 = 208

37 **18 750** First the kg should be turned into grammes: 25 × 1000 = 25 000. Divide that by 4 to find a quarter of the bag: 25 000 ÷ 4 = 6250. Then multiply 6250 by 3 to find ¾ of the bag: 6250 × 3 = 18 750

38 **30** Angles on a straight line add up to 180°. $3a + 2a + a = 6a = 180$, so $a = 180 \div 6 = 30$

39 **20** Angles on a straight line add up to 180°. $5b + 3b + b = 9b = 180$, so $b = 180 \div 9 = 20$

40 **8** Make sure you convert the 200 cm to 2 m first. 2 × 2 × 2 = 8.

Mixed Paper 4

1–3 A factor pair is a pair of numbers that multiply to make the given number.

1 **5** 3 × 5 = 15

2 **12** 1 × 12 = 12

3 **6** 2 × 6 = 12

4 **4** 1 whole = 2 halves; 2 wholes = 2 × 2 halves = 4 halves

5 **60°** Angles around a point add up to 360° ($6c = 360°$; $360° \div 6 = 60°$).

6–9 The symbol > means greater than. The symbol < means less than.

6 **True** 245 × 10 = 2450 and 24 × 100 = 2400; 2450 > 2400

7 **False** 2.45 × 100 = 245 and 24 × 10 = 240; 245 > 240

8 **False** 24.5 × 10 = 245 and 2.4 × 100 = 240; 245 > 240

9 **False** 0.245 × 100 = 24.5 and 24 × 10 = 240; 24.5 < 240

10–12 On the plan, 1 cm represents 1 m, so 2 cm represents 2 m, 3 cm represents 3 m and so on.

10 **2** Using a ruler, the length of the bed is 2 cm.

11–12 **1, 0.5** Using a ruler, the length of the wardrobe is 1 cm and the length of the stool is 0.5 cm.

13 **5 litres** 1 gallon = 4.55 litres. The closest value to 4.55 is 5 litres.

14 **31** 19 + 12 = 31

15 **16 cm²** The area of a rectangle can be found by multiplying the length by the width. In a square the length and width are the same (4 × 4 = 16).

16 **4 cm²** The square is split into 4 equal parts, 1 of which is grey; 16 ÷ 4 = 4

17 **8 cm²** The square is split into 4 equal parts, 2 of which are white; 16 ÷ 4 = 4; 4 × 2 = 8

18–20 **24, 48, 24** $\frac{1}{4}$ of the roses are red, so divide 96 by 4 to find the number of red roses (96 ÷ 4 = 24). 50% of the roses are yellow, so divide 96 by 2 to find the number of yellow roses (96 ÷ 2 = 48). Subtract the number of red roses and the number of yellow roses from 96 to find the number of pink roses (96 – 24 – 48 = 24).

21–22 **13, 11** Look for 2 numbers with a difference of 2 which add up to less than 24. For example, 10 and 12 which equals 22. We need 2 more to make this up to 24, so just increase both by 1.

23 **24** The bar for Mumbai reads 31 and the bar for Dublin reads 7 (31 – 7 = 24).

24 **17** The bar for Zurich reads –3 and the bar for Barcelona reads 14 (14 – –3 = 14 + 3 = 17).

25 **3** The bar for Moscow reads 0 and the bar for Zurich reads –3 (0 – –3 = 0 + 3 = 3).

26 **9** The bar for Helsinki reads –2 and the bar for Oslo reads –11 (–2 – – 11 = –2 + 11 = 9).

27 **92** March has 31 days, April has 30 days and May has 31 days; 31 + 30 + 31 = 92

28 **0.021** 3 × 0.007 = 0.007 + 0.007 + 0.007 = 0.021

29 **4.04** 4 × 1.01 = 1.01 + 1.01 + 1.01 + 1.01 = 4.04

30 **16** A sum is found by adding numbers together. We know that 31 is the sum, and 15 plus another number make 31. So 31 – 15 = 16

31 **3 litres** The ratio of water to concentrate is 5 : 1. There is 5 times as much water as concentrate, so multiply $\frac{1}{2}$ litre by 5 to find how much water is used ($\frac{1}{2} \times 5 = 2.5$ litres). Add the water and concentrate to find the total amount of juice (2.5 litres + 0.5 litres = 3 litres).

32 **26 cm** There are 100 centimetres in 1 metre; 2.34 m × 100 = 234 cm; 234 ÷ 9 = 26 cm

33 **50** $\frac{1}{4}$ of 48 = 48 ÷ 4 = 12; twice 19 = 38; 12 + 38 = 50

34 **9823** 10 000 – 177 = 9823

35 **22** Add up all the numbers in the Venn diagram (8 + 4 + 3 + 7 = 22).

36–37 **12, 7** Add the numbers in the oval for PE (8 + 4 = 12). Add the numbers in the oval for Art (4 + 3 = 7).

38 **4** Find the number in the overlap of the two ovals.

39–40 **10, 15** 12 out of 22 children like PE, so 22 – 12 = 10 do not. 7 out of 22 children like Art, so 22 – 7 = 15 do not.

Curveball Questions 2

1 **23** Be systematic and try all of the options. Try each number at the top vertex where the 8 is shown below. Then try each of the remaining counters where the 6 is shown.
The left side = 7 + 2 + 6 + 8 = 23
The bottom and the right side also need to equal 23.

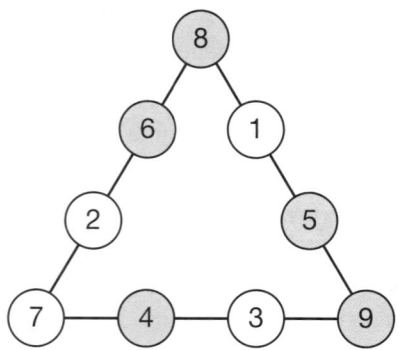

2 8 There are 4 red fruit or vegetables and 2 yellow fruit or vegetables.
Give each one a letter to identify it. Here we have A = apple, S = strawberry, R = red pepper, C = cherries, P = pear, B = banana.

A   S   R   C   P   B

The different choices that you have for 3 red fruit or vegetables and 1 yellow fruit or vegetable are: ASRP, ASRB, SRCP, SRCB, ARCP, ARCB, ASCP, ASCB.
There are 8 options.

Test Paper 1

1–6 A, B, C, D, F, G A regular polygon has all sides equal and all angles equal.

7 1 h 38 min There are 60 minutes in an hour. From 11:25 to 12:00 is 35 minutes; from 12:00 to 13:00 is 1 hour; from 13:00 to 13:03 is 3 minutes; 35 minutes + 1 hour + 3 minutes = 1 hour 38 minutes

8 $\frac{1}{9}$ The large square is split into 9 equal parts, 1 of which is dotted.

9–10 To write a number in its 'lowest terms', divide the numerator (top number) and denominator (bottom number) by the same number, making both numbers as small as possible.

9 $\frac{1}{3}$ The large square is split into 9 equal parts, 3 of which are grey; $\frac{3}{9} = \frac{1}{3}$

10 $\frac{5}{9}$ The large square is split into 9 equal parts, 5 of which are white.

11 36 cm² The area of a rectangle can be found by multiplying the length by the width ($6 \times 6 = 36$).

12–13 The whole large square has an area of 36 cm² and is split into 9 equal smaller squares, so each smaller square will have an area of $36 \div 9 = 4\,cm^2$

12 12 cm² There are 3 grey squares; $4\,cm^2 \times 3 = 12\,cm^2$

13 20 cm² There are 5 white squares; $4\,cm^2 \times 5 = 20\,cm^2$

14–19 There are 360° in a full turn. The full turn has been split into 12 equal sections, so each section is $360° \div 12 = 30°$

14 90° There are 3 sections between 12 and 3; $30 \times 3 = 90$

15 30° There is 1 section between 2 and 3; $30 \times 1 = 30$

16 60° There are 2 sections between 4 and 6; $30 \times 2 = 60$

17 90° There are 3 sections between 6 and 9; $30 \times 3 = 90$

18 180° There are 6 sections between 6 and 12; $30 \times 6 = 180$

19 30° There is 1 section between 7 and 8; $30 \times 1 = 30$

20 1998 2000 − 2 = 1998

```
  ¹2  ⁹0̸  ⁹0̸  ¹0
−              2
  1   9   9   8
```

21 413 350 + 63 = 413

```
    3  5  0
+      6  3
    4  1  3
       1
```

22 2010 1990 + 20 = 2010

```
   1  9  9  0
+         2  0
   2  0  1  0
      1  1
```

23 334 459 The smallest digit should go in the most significant place value column, so in this case the 3 will go in the hundred thousands column. The next-smallest digit should go in the next place value column, so 3 will go in the ten thousands column. Continue putting the next-smallest digit in the next place value column.

24 Three hundred and thirty-four thousand four hundred and fifty-nine Read the number from left to right starting with the hundred thousands place value column.

25 2 h 40 min There are 60 minutes in 1 hour. From 2:55 p.m. to 3 p.m. is 5 minutes. From 3 p.m. to 5 p.m. is 2 hours. From 5 p.m. to 5:35 p.m. is 35 minutes. 5 minutes + 2 hours + 35 minutes = 2 hours 40 minutes

26 59 $8 \times 7 = 56$; $56 + 3 = 59$

27 49 $9 \times 5 = 45$; $45 + 4 = 49$

28 5 $38 − 3 = 35$; $7 \times 5 = 35$

29 4 $39 − 3 = 36$; $9 \times 4 = 36$

30–33 If a shape has a line of symmetry, the sides on either side of the line will be identical.

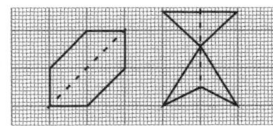 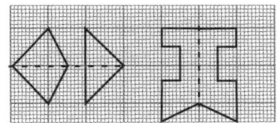

34 400 $20 \times 20 = 400$

35 13 Start with an estimate, for example $10 \times 10 = 100$. Then adjust your estimate up or down until you get to 169. For example $11 \times 11 = 121$, $12 \times 12 = 144$, $13 \times 13 = 169$

36–37 'Mixed numbers' are numbers that consist of a whole number and a fraction (for example $2\frac{1}{2}$, $4\frac{3}{4}$)

36 $1\frac{1}{10}$ $3 = \frac{30}{10}$; $1\frac{9}{10} = \frac{19}{10}$; $\frac{30}{10} − \frac{19}{10} = \frac{11}{10} = 1\frac{1}{10}$

37 $2\frac{6}{7}$ $5 = \frac{35}{7}$; $2\frac{1}{7} = \frac{15}{7}$; $\frac{35}{7} − \frac{15}{7} = \frac{20}{7} = 2\frac{6}{7}$

38 85 cm There are 100 centimetres in 1 metre; $3.4\,m \times 100 = 340\,cm$. A square has 4 equal sides; $340\,cm \div 4 = 85\,cm$

39 **16.19** $7.69 + 4.82 + 3.68 = 16.19$

```
        7  ·  6  9
        4  ·  8  2
    +   3  ·  6  8
    ─────────────────
    1   6  ·  1  9
        2     1
```

40 **100** The bar chart shows that 100 people came on Monday.

41 **90** The bar chart shows that 90 people came on Wednesday.

42 **Wednesday** The lowest bar is on Wednesday.

43 **630** $100 + 120 + 90 + 150 + 170 = 630$

44 **121** ($11\,cm \times 11\,cm = 121\,cm^2$)

45 **6th or sixth** Page 1 has lines 1–20; page 2 has lines 21–40; page 3 has lines 41–60; page 4 has lines 61–80; page 5 has lines 81–100; page 6 has lines 101–120. Therefore, line 110 is on page 6.

46 **68** $52 - 16 = 36$; $2 \times 16 = 32$; $36 + 32 = 68$

47 **103 500** $345 \times 3 = 1035$; $1035 \times 100 = 103\,500$

48 $\frac{2}{5}$ $0.4 = \frac{4}{10} = \frac{2}{5}$

49 $\frac{1}{4}$ $0.25 = \frac{25}{100} = \frac{1}{4}$

50 $\frac{9}{10}$ $0.9 = \frac{9}{10}$

51 $\frac{3}{100}$ $0.03 = \frac{3}{100}$

52 $\frac{1}{100}$ $0.01 = \frac{1}{100}$

53 $\frac{7}{100}$ $0.07 = \frac{7}{100}$

54–57 **1 and 27, 3 and 9** A factor pair is a pair of numbers that multiply to make the given number. $1 \times 27 = 27$; $3 \times 9 = 27$

58 **2** $28 \div 7 = 4$; $8 \div 4 = 2$

59 **5** $36 \div 9 = 4$; $20 \div 4 = 5$

60 **48** $54 \div 9 = 6$; $6 \times 8 = 48$

61 **2 cm** $139.5 - 137.5 = 2\,cm$

62 **3.5 cm or $3\frac{1}{2}$ cm** $139 - 135.5 = 3.5\,cm$

63 **2.5 cm or $2\frac{1}{2}$ cm** $137.5 - 135 = 2.5\,cm$

64 **2.5 cm or $2\frac{1}{2}$ cm** $137 - 134.5 = 2.5\,cm$

65–66 **80, 120** Divide by 5 to find $\frac{1}{5}$ ($200 \div 5 = 40$) and multiply by 2 to find $\frac{2}{5}$ ($40 \times 2 = 80$); there are 80 girls. Subtract the number of girls from the total to find the number of boys ($200 - 80 = 120$).

67 $\frac{5}{16}$ The circle is split into 16 equal sections, 5 of which are dotted.

68 $\frac{3}{16}$ The circle is split into 16 equal sections, 3 of which are grey.

69 $\frac{7}{16}$ The circle is split into 16 equal sections, 7 of which are unshaded.

70 $\frac{1}{2}$ There are 5 dotted sections and 3 grey sections; $5 + 3 = 8$; $\frac{8}{16} = \frac{1}{2}$

71 **3 litres** The ratio of water to concentrate is 4 : 1. There is 4 times as much water as concentrate, so multiply 0.6 litres by 4 to find how much water is used ($4 \times 0.6 = 2.4$ litres). Add the water and concentrate find the total amount of juice (2.4 litres + 0.6 litres = 3 litres).

72 **11:04** Add 11 minutes to 10:53 (10:53 to 11:00 is 7 minutes; 11:00 to 11:04 is 4 minutes = 11:04).

73–76 **2.222, 2.22, 2.2, 2.02** To order the decimals, look at the ones first, then the tenths, then the hundredths and then the thousandths. Remember that 2.2 is the same as 2.20 or 2.200.

77 **10 989** $11\,000 - 11 = 10\,989$

```
    1  ⁰1̶  ⁹0̶  ⁹0̶  ¹0
  –            1   1
  ─────────────────────
    1  0   9   8   9
```

78 **3.006 kg** $300 + 500 + 200 + 2 = 1002$, $1002 \times 3 = 3006\,g$; $3006\,g = 3.006\,kg$

79–80 **4, 12** $x \times x \times 3x = 192$; so $3 \times x^3 = 192$ and $x^3 = 192 \div 3 = 64$, $4^3 = 64$ So the width is 4 cm and the length is triple that, $4 \times 4 \times 12 = 192$

Test Paper 2

1 **48.8** $19.1\,km + 29.7\,km = 48.8\,km$

2 **56.9** $27.2\,km + 29.7\,km = 56.9\,km$

3 **44.5** $25.4\,km + 19.1\,km = 44.5\,km$

4 **52.6** $25.4\,km + 27.2\,km = 52.6\,km$

5 **16** $4 \times 4 = 16$

6 **49** $7^2 = 7 \times 7 = 49$

7 **25** $200 \div 8 = 25$

8 **8** A product is found by multiplying numbers together ($6 \times 7 = 42$; $50 - 42 = 8$).

9 **1.5 km** 1 mile = 1.61 km. The closest value to 1.61 is 1.5.

10–18 A face is a flat surface of a 3D shape, an edge is the straight line where 2 faces meet and a vertex is a corner where 2 or more faces meet.

	A	B	C
Number of faces	6	5	5
Number of vertices	8	6	5
Number of edges	12	9	8

19 $\frac{29}{100}$ $\frac{24}{100} + \frac{13}{100} - \frac{8}{100} = \frac{29}{100}$

20 **200 less** $478 - 100 = 378$; $199 - 100 = 99$; $378 + 99 = 477$; 477 is 200 less than 677.

21 **the same** $478 - 100 = 378$; $199 - 100 = 99$; $378 - 99 = 279$

22 **31** 1 whole = 4 quarters; $7 + \frac{3}{4} = 7 \times 4$ quarters + 3 quarters = 28 quarters + 3 quarters = 31 quarters

23 **9400** $47 \times 2 = 94$; $94 \times 100 = 9400$

24 **89** Noon is 12:00. From 12:00 to 13:00 is 1 hour = 60 minutes; from 13:00 to 13:29 is 29 minutes; $60 + 29 = 89$

25 **38** There are 7 days in a week; $266 \div 7 = 38$

26–33 An acute angle is less than 90°. A right angle is exactly 90°. An obtuse angle is greater than 90° but less than 180°. A reflex angle is greater than 180°.

26–27 **acute, 40°**

28–29 **obtuse, 100°**

30–31 **reflex, 230°**

32–33 **acute, 60°**

34–36 There are different strategies for solving each of these questions, here is one method:

34 **16.05**

```
      7 . 4 9
  +   8 . 5 6
  ─────────────
    1 6 . 0 5
        1   1
```

35 **4.34**

```
      1 . 7 8
  +   2 . 5 6
  ─────────────
      4 . 3 4
        1   1
```

36 **4.05**

```
      1 . 6 8
  +   2 . 3 7
  ─────────────
      4 . 0 5
        1   1
```

37 **16** 3 × 4 = 12 boys, so there are 4 lots of 3 boys. Therefore there will be 4 lots of 4 girls (4 × 4 = 16).

38 **9** 4 × 3 = 12 girls, so there are 3 lots of 4 girls. Therefore there will be 3 lots of 3 boys (3 × 3 = 9).

39 **49** In the first youth club there are 12 boys and 16 girls. At the second youth club there are 9 boys and 12 girls. 12 + 16 + 9 + 12 = 49

40 **40p** £3.00 = 300p; 4 × 65p = 260p; 300p – 260p = 40p

41–42 There are 10 increments between 0 and 1 litre. There are 1000 millilitres in 1 litre. Divide 1000 ml by the number of increments (1000 ÷ 10 = 100 ml). So each increment represents 100 ml.

41 **300 ml**

42 **500 ml**

43–45 Subtract the amount in the jug from 1000 ml.

43 **300 ml** 1000 – 700 = 300

44 **700 ml** 1000 – 300 = 700

45 **500 ml** 1000 – 500 = 500

46 **2 h 24 min** There are 60 minutes in an hour. 07:49 to 08:00 is 11 minutes; 08:00 to 10:00 is 2 hours; 10:00 to 10:13 is 13 minutes; 11 minutes + 2 hours + 13 minutes = 2 hours 24 minutes

47 **14 m** The perimeter of a rectangle can be found by adding up the 2 lengths and the 2 widths. The length of the bathroom is 4 m. Using a ruler, measure the width of the bathroom. It is 6 cm; 2 cm represents 1 m, so 6 cm represents 3 m. 4 m + 3 m + 4 m + 3 m = 14 m

48 **48** The area of a rectangle can be found by multiplying the length by the width. There are 100 centimetres in 1 metre, so the area of the bathroom is 400 cm × 300 cm = 120 000 cm². The area of one tile is 50 cm × 50 cm = 2500 cm². Divide the area of the bathroom by the area of one tile to find how many will fit (120 000 ÷ 2500 = 48).

49 **40** Using a ruler to measure, the width of the bath is 2 cm; 2 cm represents 1 m. The area of the bath is 200 cm × 100 cm = 20 000 cm². The area of one tile is 50 cm × 50 cm = 2500 cm². 20 000 ÷ 2500 = 8, so 8 tiles would be under bath; 48 – 8 = 40

50 **2 m²** 2 m × 1 m = 2 m²

51 **12 m²** 4 m × 3 m = 12 m²

52–55 When plotting coordinates on a grid, use the rule 'along the corridor and up the stairs' to remember to go horizontal, then vertical.

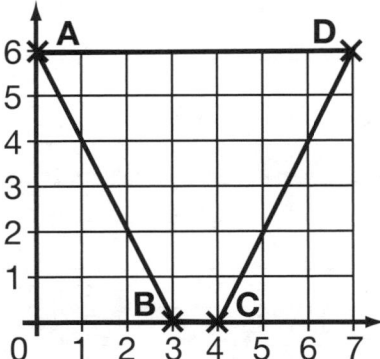

56 **Quadrilateral** A quadrilateral has 4 sides. A pentagon has 5 sides.

57 **Trapezium** A trapezium has 1 pair of parallel sides.

58

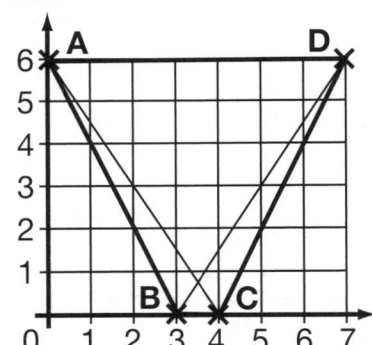

59 **1** If a shape has a line of symmetry, the sides on either side of the line will be identical.

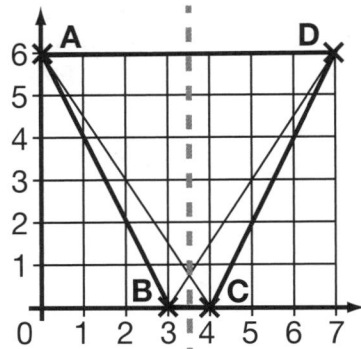

60 52 $28 \div 2 = 14$; $19 \times 2 = 38$; $14 + 38 = 52$

61–65 To divide by 100, place the numbers in a decimal grid using hundreds, tens, ones, tenths, hundredths, thousandths, etc. Reduce a number by 100 by moving it 2 places to the right.

61 0.0355

Th	H	T	O	.	t	h	th	tth
			3	.	5	5		
			0	.	0	3	5	5

62 0.0305

Th	H	T	U	.	t	h	th	tth
			3	.	0	5		
			0	.	0	3	0	5

63 0.305

Th	H	T	U	.	t	h	th	tth
		3	0	.	5			
			0	.	3	0	5	

64 3.035

Th	H	T	U	.	t	h	th	tth
	3	0	3	.	5			
			3	.	0	3	5	

65 30.5

Th	H	T	U	.	t	h	th	tth
3	0	5	0	.				
		3	0	.	5			

66 25 £6 = 600p; 600 ÷ 24 = 25

67 27 Divide 30 by 10 to find $\frac{1}{10}$ (30 ÷ 10 = 3). Subtract this from 30 to find $\frac{9}{10}$ (30 – 3 = 27).

68 7 cm² Picture the shape as 2 rectangles. The left-hand rectangle is 1 cm wide and 5 cm high. Multiply these two numbers to get the area (1 cm × 5 cm = 5 cm²). Now find the area of the right-hand rectangle. The total width of the shape is 3 cm and the left-hand rectangle is 1 cm wide, so the right-hand rectangle must be 2 cm wide (3 cm – 1 cm = 2 cm). The rectangle is 1 cm high, so multiplying the length and width gives 2 cm². Add the areas of the 2 rectangles to get the total area (5 cm² + 2 cm² = 7 cm²).

69 9 cm² Picture the shape as 2 rectangles. The top rectangle is 5 cm wide and 1 cm high. Multiply these two numbers to get the area (5 cm × 1 cm = 5 cm²). The bottom rectangle is 1 cm wide and 4 cm high. Multiply these two numbers to get the area (1 cm × 4 cm = 4 cm²). Add the areas of the 2 rectangles to get the total area (5 cm² + 4 cm² = 9 cm²).

70 9 cm² Picture the shape as 3 rectangles. The central rectangle is 1 cm wide and 5 cm high (XY). Multiply these two numbers to get the area (1 cm × 5 cm = 5 cm²). Now find the area of the left-hand and right-hand rectangles, which are the same size. The total width of the shape is 5 cm (RS) and the central rectangle is 1 cm wide, so the width of the left-hand and right-hand rectangle must be 2 cm each (5 cm – 1 cm = 4 cm and 4 cm ÷ 2 = 2 cm). The rectangles are both 1 cm high, so multiplying the length and width gives 2 cm². Add the areas of the 3 rectangles to get the total area (5 cm² + 2 cm² + 2 cm² = 9 cm²).

71 58.86 6.54 × 9 = 58.86

```
        6 . 5 4
    ×         9
    ---------------
      5 8 . 8 6
      5 4   3
```

72 16.25 or 16.250 9.500 + 6.750 = 16.25

```
      9 . 5 0 0
  +   6 . 7 5 0
  ---------------
    1 6 . 2 5 0
        1
```

73 b abbr is a repeating pattern of 4 letters. Therefore, a will be the first, fifth and ninth symbol. The eleventh symbol will be 2 symbols on from the ninth, which is b.

74 o The ninth letter in the pattern is t. There is one other t earlier in the pattern, which is followed by o. So the tenth letter must be o.

75 x xxyzz is a repeating pattern of 5 letters. Therefore, x will be the first and second letter, the sixth and seventh letter, the eleventh and twelfth letter, and the sixteenth and seventeenth letter.

76 23 400 The 3 tens in 23 432 rounds down to 23 400.

77 47 900 The 7 tens in 47 874 rounds up to 47 900.

78 35 200 The 5 tens in 35 153 rounds up to 35 200.

79 77 100 The 7 tens in 77 077 rounds up to 77 100.

80 19 200 The 9 tens in 19 191 rounds up to 19 200.